TESTIMONIALS

"As a fertility expert (and someone who has the quote "bringing hope to life" in my email signature), I love the message that Jenny Lowe shares in *Saved by Hope*. The fertility journey often takes a patient on many twists and turns, and in this book we learn about Jenny navigating infertility, cancer, and surrogacy on her path to becoming a mother. Her experiences make her a powerful guide for any reader, and she offers an inspired perspective of what it can look like to grow your family in today's world. In sharing her story with humor and authenticity, Jenny is helping to break down the stigmas of infertility. Her story encourages everyone going through treatment to keep going, and to hold on to hope. Her book is a lovely guide for anyone looking for personal guidance, a community, or sense of hope in challenging times."

—Dr. Aimee Eyvazzadeh MD, MPH

"I couldn't flip through the pages quickly enough! I was gripped from the very beginning, eager to find out what happened. The writing is raw, moving, and beautifully illustrated. I felt like I had a front-row seat to this inspiring story of love, loss, and what true resilience looks like.

This is book is inspirational and full of hope as Jenny takes readers on a journey through various challenges in life. She shows readers how to create hope in life even when the odds feel stacked against you. Thank you, Jenny, for birthing this beautiful book into the World.

I recommend this book for those looking for hope in the midst of uncertainty. I will be sharing this book with my patients, and can see it being a huge asset in fertility clinics, and oncology units across the World. Grab your copy today, I promise you will leave this book with a new perspective on life, love, and what true hope looks like."

—**Andrea Blindt, Fertility specialized registered nurse, 4x international best-selling author, life and mindset coach**

"Jenny shares the honest, raw and emotional journey that is infertility. I was gripped from the first chapter and felt enthralled reading her account of fertility treatments, cancer, surgeries, miscarriage and surrogacy— all of which were on her path to motherhood. This book so beautifully describes the determination, heartbreak and perseverance that is infertility and demonstrates the hope that is possible when you never give up."

—**Ariel Taylor, Fertility Therapist, experienced surrogate**

"Jenny's story of determination in the midst of illness, infertility, and surrogacy will provide information and inspiration to any who find themselves on a similar path to parenthood. *Saved by Hope* reminds us that through perseverance in the face of trial and with the love and support of family, we, too, can find hope to overcome obstacles that seem insurmountable."

—**Dr. Spencer Barney MD, FACOG: OBGYN**

"At a time when you might feel most alone, Lowe's *Saved by Hope* is a friend, a lifeline and a beacon of light. Any woman going through fertility treatments should read this book."

—**Sara Connell bestselling author of *Bringing in Finn***

"*Saved By Hope* is a beautiful and raw memoir of Jenny's journey to becoming a mother. Her ability to be vulnerable and open up about such a pivotal moment in her life will undoubtedly tug at your heart. Jenny shares her story in a way that makes you feel you are right there with her, through the good news and the bad. It's an admirable chronicle of hope, strength and courage."
—**Jaimie Selwa, Author of** *First There Was Me, The Journey to You*

"Jenny's story is both heartbreaking and inspirational. While many would have crumbled, Jenny shows us that we can sustain and persist through life's most challenging times."
—**Monique Farook, founder,** *Infertility and Me* **Podcast**

"Jenny's honest approach to her writing takes you straight into the emotional rollercoaster of infertility and how we have to manage this overwhelming and invasive life experience as life just goes on. The calls keep coming delivering more bad news, that you just have to take in your stride and carry on. Jenny takes you on the journey through her and James' experience of dealing with such news, that is all so unfair, and she manages to share all this in such a caring and compelling way that you can't put the book down. Her story is one of such resilience and I know it will help so many people, so thank you Jenny for sharing."
—**Natalie Silverman, founder of** *The Fertility Podcast*, **co-founder of Fertility Matters at Work**

"The vulnerability that Jenny shows by taking us on her raw but 'hopeful' journey to become a mother and create a family for her and her husband reminds us that nothing should be taken for granted. It's safe to say that we have all been touched by infertility at some point, but this book reminds us that it can happen to anyone and that if and when it does you are not on an island alone dealing with it. The power of Jenny's story is proof that we are all stronger than we think."
—**Jade Elliott, Morning News Anchor, KUTV and Host of the** *Baby Your Baby* **Podcast**

SAVED
BY
HOPE

SAVED

— BY —

HOPE

JENNY LOWE

MUSE
LITERARY

CHICAGO·NEWYORK·PARIS·ROME

Printed in the United States of America

Paperback ISBN: 978-1-958714-31-7
Ebook ISBN: 978-1-958714-32-4
Hardcover ISBN: 978-1-958714-30-0

Library of Congress Control Number: 2022945645

CHICAGO · NEW YORK · PARIS · ROME
Muse Literary
3319 N. Cicero Avenue

Chicago IL 60641-9998

DEDICATIONS

For my Little Bird
and the feathers forever perched in my soul.
Three squeezes.

NOTE TO READERS

Saved By Hope includes QR codes that direct readers to online galleries containing photos and videos of topics discussed throughout various chapters.

Beginning with Chapter 4, readers can scan the QR code to follow along.

*"Hope is the thing with feathers
that perches in the soul."*

—Emily Dickinson

PROLOGUE

I t was a few days before Christmas in 2019. My husband and I, along with my brother and his wife, anxiously waited in an exam room for our nurse to return with her colleague. My brother paced back and forth as his wife lay on the table with only a thin blanket covering her torso.

I gazed off, trying desperately to avoid even the shortest moment of eye contact. I feared the slightest glance would fracture the composure I battled internally to maintain. I had no control over what was happening but felt the need to appear less affected by the weight of it. After all, I had put my sister-in-law in this situation to begin with. Within moments, we'd find out if the baby she was carrying, my baby, still had a heartbeat. I fought back tears each time I contemplated what this moment could mean for my family's future.

Holiday music played in the background, inviting me to have a holly, jolly Christmas. *What a stupid song.* I tapped my foot along to the beat anyway, although I sure couldn't pretend this was the happiest time of year. I wasn't thinking about the presents under our tree or the holiday traditions we had started making. All I could picture was the flickering image of a heartbeat I'd seen on a black and white screen four days prior, after learning my sister-in-law had started bleeding—a flicker we desperately hoped could still be found after she was placed on bed rest, only six weeks pregnant.

After what felt like an eternity, our nurse finally reentered the room, her counterpart close behind. Ordinarily I would have expected to see our doctor, but due to the clinic double-booking him, combined with the urgent nature of our visit, his nurse had come in his place. After five minutes of watching her search diligently for a heartbeat, she had left the room to find someone who could provide a second set of eyes.

Knowing we were there to see if our baby was still alive, the new nurse quickly made her way to the ultrasound machine, avoiding small talk. The familiar sound of latex snapped her wrists, and she wheeled her squeaky chair over to the exam table.

"Let's see what we can find," she said, squirting lube on the ultrasound wand.

My wedding ring pressed deeply into my skin as my husband squeezed my left hand. My right hand tightly grasped the softly shaking hand of my sister-in-law, our heartbeats pulsing through our fingers.

My focus shifted between the monitor and the expression on the nurse's face as she searched for a sign of life. She bit her bottom lip, and I soon felt my teeth sinking into my own. I sat at the edge of my seat, knowing one small movement would put me on the floor.

*Come on, dammit. Please...*I exhaled as I begged. *Find my baby.*

CHAPTER 1

When I was young, I loved being the center of attention. I often stood on our yellow stone fireplace hearth, hairbrush as a microphone in my hand, singing for anyone who would listen. I daydreamed about being a pop star and traveling the world, filling arenas with thousands of fans.

At eight years old, my mom enrolled me in figure skating lessons at the local ice rink. For six years I competed against other kids with my same skill set. I envisioned myself waving from the "kiss and cry" area at the Olympics, telling my family how much I loved and missed them. In both scenarios, I wore sparkly leotards, and everyone was there to see me. As I got older and my fantastical dreams became more realistic, I wondered how much money I'd make, where I would live, and whom I would marry. Surprisingly, I never thought about having kids. I assumed I would probably have them one day, but the maternal instinct everyone talked about wasn't something I felt.

Born and raised in Utah, I was a member of the Church of Jesus Christ of Latter-day Saints, also known as Mormon. In this faith community it isn't uncommon for couples to date and get married at a young age. I was no exception. At nineteen years old, I got married and was excited to finally see how the rest of my life would unfold.

Unfortunately, after only eighteen short months, it became clear the marriage wasn't working. I had to accept, no matter the consequence and despite every effort to endure, that I'd failed. At the age of twenty-one, I found myself a divorcee. I was barely old enough to get into a bar, yet somehow making the decision to end a marriage I thought was supposed to last forever.

After getting divorced, I strongly hoped I'd put the hardest years and trials behind me. I hate to call anything "20/20," but hindsight is just that. As each year passed, I grew a little wiser and more skeptical about happiness. I started to believe I might not experience it in the way I'd I always hoped I would. It felt as though I had to fight harder than others to prove I still deserved good things to happen to me.

After what felt like a lifetime of heartache and self-discovery, I finally found the happiness I deserved. In October 2016, at the age of thirty-two, I stood in front of James, a former Starbucks barista I'd dated on and off since 2009, and vowed to spend the rest of my life with him. James and I had been through some dramatic ups and downs over the years, but we had persevered. I believed if we could overcome some of the struggles and failures our relationship had faced, we could overcome anything.

James and I had an eventful first year of marriage. We built our first home and did a lot of traveling. We drank champagne outside the Colosseum in Rome, got lost in the streets of Venice, kissed atop the Eiffel Tower, saw Romeo and Juliet at the Globe in London, and jumped off a pirate ship in Aruba. Not long after celebrating our one-year anniversary, we decided it was time to start trying to have a baby.

We had watched several of our friends and family members have kids and knew our ability to easily pick up and go on a vacation or to dinner and the bar on a Friday night would become more difficult and less frequent. I also expected introducing a baby into our lives would create a level of chaos I was scared I wouldn't know how to handle, having always been one to crave control.

However, we were finally in a place emotionally and financially to responsibly bring a child into this world, outweighing any fears we had about the unexpected. Not to mention, I wasn't getting any younger.

I believed getting pregnant would be quick and easy. Other than an early miscarriage my older sister had faced before going on to have a healthy pregnancy, I didn't know much about infertility, nor did I think it would affect me. I was more concerned about an unexpected pregnancy and had taken birth control pills religiously starting at the age of eighteen.

Growing up in the Mormon faith, we were taught premarital sex was a sin and could lead to having a child out of wedlock. Even though I'd left the faith in my early twenties, this still resonated with me. I'd seen that getting pregnant didn't always happen when someone expected or wanted it, and I was sure when I purposefully started trying it would happen without issue. I was wrong.

I stopped taking my pills at the end of November 2017. Turning off my nightly ten-p.m. alarm and choosing not to refill my prescription was a choice I consciously made for the first time in my life. Now, here we were, just another couple "trying" to have a baby. It felt like a cruel twist in life; the longer we waited and the more prepared we were emotionally, physically, and financially, the harder it might be.

Something I had never really grasped was how perfectly timed everything had to be to become pregnant. I knew creating life was a miraculous thing but didn't understand the intricacies of the science behind it. It started to become clear it wasn't as simple as I thought.

For nearly six months, I devoutly monitored my cycle and ovulation, downloading not only one, but three of the most highly-rated tracking apps on my phone. At first, it was an exhilarating feeling knowing we were working toward something we had both tried to avoid for so many years. I was excited to finally get my chance to see the "plus sign" on a pregnancy test.

As the first month came and went, so did another period. I expected it might take a month or two for the years of birth control to exit my system, something I'd heard from many sources was a possibility. But when month three resulted in yet another period, I started to become a bit discouraged.

The illusion of getting pregnant on a beach after a romantic evening of wining and dining started to fade in my mind. Intimacy was losing its allure as I started setting alarms for sex. I avoided making sexual advances toward James, and dismissed any from him, when the timing wasn't right.

"No, now isn't the right time. We have two more hours," I would say, pulling away from a lingering kiss or a touch on my thigh.

Much like Pavlov's dogs, I responded the instant I heard the chime on my phone indicating the optimal window was upon us. I read online we needed to save up James' sperm between sex, but if we waited too long, it could be less effective.

I even bought into old wives' tales about positions during and after intercourse that could help his sperm and my egg meet more naturally. I felt somewhat ridiculous lying on my back, legs in the air, trying to ensure gravity was doing its part. I also knew it could take months or years to conceive. This tested my patience, which unfortunately was not one of my strengths.

By May 2018, about to turn thirty-four, I decided to talk to my doctor. It had been nearly six months with no luck. I started looking for a new obstetrician (OB) and grew frustrated as everyone had wait lists longer than three months.

"Why don't you just go to the same one you've been going to?" James asked, hearing me conclude my fifth call.

"Don't you remember how awful my last visit was?" I asked, knowing he wouldn't.

A year prior, I tested positive for human papillomavirus (HPV), my first ever abnormal pap result. Knowing HPV can be an early sign of cervical cancer, my doctor suggested a loop electrosurgical excision procedure, known as a LEEP. I made the mistake of finding a YouTube video prior to having it done. Lying on the table, every muscle in my body tightened. My doctor held an instrument that looked like a tongue scraper used to help with bad breath. Only, this one was connected to an electrical current.

"I am going to swab your cervix with a vinegar solution so I can see where the abnormal cells are," she said, dabbing a long swab with liquid. Moments later, she held up a syringe and needle. "I'm going to numb the area now, try and relax."

Relax? How the hell am I supposed to relax when you are about to stick a needle into my vagina?

"I can see someone does their Kegel exercises," she said. I took it as a compliment, as well as an indication I needed to loosen up.

"I really need you to hold still. I am going to burn the abnormal tissue off." She held the buzzing instrument in her hand. "It is important you don't flinch."

What the actual fuck? Every single muscle in my body was rigid as I tried to stay as still as possible. Despite being numb, I could feel the instrument enter my body and immediately did the exact opposite of what she had instructed. I flinched. I never knew it possible to have a third-degree burn on your vaginal wall, but I was made painfully aware at that moment. A kind nurse came over and took my hand, helping calm me just enough to get through the remainder of the procedure.

"All done," the doctor said, throwing away the blood-stained gauze and wipes she had used to clean up. I immediately started crying when she left the room. Tears streamed down my face as I searched for my underwear and a pad.

A cup full of reddish-tinted liquid sat on the metal stand next to the exam table. I picked it up, wiping the snot running from my nose with my sleeve. A tiny piece of tissue bobbed inside. My abnormal, HPV-ridden cervical tissue would soon be on its way to pathology to test for cancer. I examined it for a moment, disgusted and intrigued, before leaving the room. One week later, my vagina mostly healed, the results came back negative.

I finally found an OB that didn't have a waiting list and made an appointment. Most of the time, my first encounter with a new doctor was an introduction as they entered the room, followed quickly by gloves on, speculum in. I didn't expect to receive any kind of special treatment, but the fact I'd become accustomed to this routine was disheartening. However, to my surprise, my first visit with Dr. Barney, was the exact opposite.

After checking in, I was led into an office, rather than an exam room. The walls were decorated with various degrees, accolades, and family photos. Thank-you notes with photos of happy, smiling babies were pinned on an overflowing cork board. A large, neatly organized desk took up most of the open space, except for a small loveseat and two chairs, where I was asked to sit and wait.

It felt like a scene from a movie, waiting for the doctor to come in and inevitably share a devastating diagnosis. *If these walls could talk.* After only a few short moments, a man dressed in scrubs and a white coat entered. I was pleasantly surprised as he introduced himself and sat for ten minutes to discuss my medical history. His effort to understand my past as well as the reason for being there felt unfamiliar to me.

When we finished talking, I was led to the exam room where the familiarity finally kicked in. These rooms always had an old feel to them. Everything looked as though it was built or purchased in the 1980s, even down to the models of the cervix and ovaries displayed on the counter. I wondered how many people had picked them up for a better look, and embarrassed, set them down when the doctor came in.

"Everything looks normal," Dr. Barney said, fully aware I'd gone through a LEEP only a year before. "I think because you've been trying to conceive for six months and because of your age, I suggest you begin fertility testing."

Although a little surprised that we would be seeing a fertility specialist so soon, I was relieved we didn't have to wait any longer. At his recommendation, James and I started down a road we hadn't envisioned we would ever need to travel, let alone one that would save my life.

CHAPTER 2

S hortly after my visit with Dr. Barney, I made an appointment to see a fertility specialist. At the time, I had several coworkers who had experienced reproductive issues. It was rather common, when going into the break room for a coffee refill, to overhear colleagues talking about sperm, eggs, and ovaries. I was invited into these conversations and was surprised at how casually this issue was being discussed in such an open space.

I'd always assumed conversations about infertility were considered more private by those involved, which is probably why I knew so little about it. It became increasingly clear infertility was not something someone should feel ashamed of. I felt anger bubbling, knowing the stigma tied to it caused people not to share their experiences. I could only imagine how lonely and isolating it might feel without others' support.

I learned several of my colleagues were patients at the same clinic, with nothing but good things to say about their experiences. They had all ended up with babies after going through treatment, and that was all I needed to hear.

We arrived at our first appointment feeling nervous and uncertain of what to expect. Being nosey in nature, I found it hard not to look around at the other patients in the waiting room and wonder what had brought them to the clinic. *What is wrong with that woman's uterus? Does that man have good sperm? How long has that couple been trying?* My curious gaze led to either a polite, yet commiserating smile, or complete avoidance of eye contact.

"Mrs. Lowe?" the receptionist called out. As I approached her desk, I glanced at the clock to see we had been waiting just under an hour. "Dr. Hall is a bit behind. As an apology for the inconvenience, we have some ten-dollar vouchers to be used here at the clinic toward any future procedure."

I looked at the papers now in my hand, confused and annoyed. "Do you know how far behind he is?" I asked.

"No, unfortunately we don't, just that he is running late. Are you okay to continue waiting?" she asked politely. She had to know I wasn't about to leave after having already waited this long.

"Yes, as long as we aren't waiting another hour," I answered, more harshly than she deserved. I walked back to my seat and handed the papers to James, who examined them curiously.

"Apparently they're handing out coupons," I said, sarcastically.

After waiting another thirty minutes, a nurse finally called for us. It was not a great start to meeting the man with whom we were entrusting our fertility. Something about him being late seemed painfully ironic. We entered his office, and I felt all of my annoyances disappear as I came face to face with a gentle, soft-spoken man in his early fifties.

"Hello, I am Dr. Hall," he said, his handshake strong and his skin soft. "Sorry for the delay. Please come in and take a seat."

After a lengthy self-introduction, he began discussing the common difficulties couples face when trying to conceive. From various complications within the female anatomy to possible issues with sperm, there didn't seem to be a shortage of options.

"Because the female reproductive system is far more complex than the male's, the first step is usually to determine if there are problems with the sperm, as it is easy to collect," he said, walking over to his bookshelf and pulling out a thick book. He placed it on the table, with a loud thud, and thumbed through the pages. I never knew sperm could be so complicated and thought the only thing tested was semen volume and sperm count. I had no idea other characteristics affected their viability.

"Here are pictures of the morphology, or the different shapes and sizes of a sperm," he said, pointing to an image of a sperm with two heads and then another with one unusually large head. "If the head of a sperm has an abnormal shape, it most likely won't be strong enough to break through the shell of an egg, and if somehow it did, the pregnancy would most likely lead to miscarriage or severe birth defects," he explained.

In that moment, it became clear. Size does matter.

Next in his sperm bible, he flipped to a page showing various pictures illustrating the direction in which sperm should be swimming.

"The movement of sperm is known as motility, and we want to see at least forty percent of the sperm swimming in a mostly straight line or in large circles."

I always thought sperm looked as depicted in a recent *Simpsons* rerun I'd watched. A petri dish contained Homer's frantic sperm bumping into one another under a microscope. Clearly, his motility was shit.

"Once we have a semen sample from James, our andrologist will evaluate the sperm more closely under a microscope." To our unexpected amusement, he then added a touch of color. "Think of it this way," he said. "The andrologist's job is to wrangle the best sperm, much like wrangling a bull, in what I like to call the sperm rodeo." He smiled ear to ear. I wondered how many times he had made that joke.

James and I couldn't help but laugh. Something about this sweet man describing such a scientific process in this colorful way offered a moment of relief during what could otherwise be a heavy conversation.

"How did you feel about that?" I asked as we left the appointment.

"Obviously I don't want to find out I'm the cause of our infertility," he replied. "But if that turns out to be the case, I promise I'll do everything I can to ensure we find a resolution." I knew I'd married a man who would always take care of me and my family, and slept a little easier that night.

James went in a few days later to give a semen sample. Although I'd been told I could attend, I decided against it, certain my presence would make it even more stressful.

"How was it?" I asked when he called from the car on his drive home.

"That was more awkward than I expected it to be," he said. "Did you know they offer a service that someone will come in and help if you need it?"

"WHAT?" I blurted out.

"Yeah, it was so strange. Don't worry, though, I didn't do it. They said insurance doesn't cover it."

"Are you fucking kidding me?" I was appalled and confused how this could even be legal.

"Yes, I am kidding you, duh! Could you imagine?" He laughed. I could tell he was proud I'd fallen for his absurd joke.

"Oh my God, you are such a butthole," I said, embarrassed by my gullibility. "I wanted to know what the hell kind of operation they run over there."

"I mean, how do you think it went? I had to 'knock one out' on command." He chuckled. "And I was in my head the whole time so I don't know how well I performed."

He had performed just fine, and a week later, we were back in the waiting room to discuss results with Dr. Hall.

"Jenny Lowe?" I looked up to see the receptionist waving her hand, then glanced at the clock. Dr. Hall was already forty-five minutes late.

Lucky me, more coupons. I made my way to the desk, letting out a frustrated sigh. I was given two more ten dollar vouchers and immediately wadded them up into my sweater pocket.

After another forty-five minutes, we were led back to Dr. Hall's office, both visibly annoyed over the delay. All we had done until this point was wait—wait for ovulation, wait to take a pregnancy test, wait for test results. I was tired of waiting.

After ten minutes of re-explaining how sperm is tested, he slid a piece of paper in front of us that had a lot of numbers on it. He spent the next thirty minutes walking us through what they meant.

James was producing an above-average amount of sperm, and the motility, or direction, they swam in was normal. However, his test showed a high number of abnormally-shaped sperm, and as a result, they were likely having difficulty penetrating my egg.

"This is very common. In fact, only about four to ten percent of sperm is shaped normally," he assured us. We felt better knowing our problem was the most common. Nonetheless, I could tell James was disappointed to hear his sperm contributed to our struggle.

Although we had some answers, Dr. Hall suggested moving forward with a few tests on me. I was frustrated when we left the appointment. If I'd known the intent was to have me tested, regardless of James' results, I would have scheduled appointments sooner. Again, I was left waiting.

Two weeks later, I went in to have a hysterosalpingogram, or HSG. This was typically the first fertility test completed on women, other than a simple blood draw. As if I hadn't already felt uninformed about infertility, I was constantly being reminded of my ignorance.

I'd thought testing could all be done at once, with a simple test. Take some blood, get a urine sample, and voilà, you had answers. Instead, it was a "hurry up and wait" situation, a phrase I quickly grew to resent. Most tests could only be done at certain times during my monthly cycle. I hadn't known the result from a test on day sixteen would lead to a second test that could only be done on day four, followed by another test on day twenty. There are few things more discouraging when eagerly trying to start a family than being told to wait one more month to take more tests that will provide only one more answer.

An HSG evaluates the inside of the uterus and fallopian tubes for abnormalities. Not knowing what to expect, I was led into a large exam room full of several intimidating tools and machines. My heart began to race, and my palms became dewy with sweat. I undressed and waited for the doctor. I was flooded with vivid and painful memories of my LEEP a year and a half prior that had left me mentally and physically scarred for life.

I don't know if I can do this. My nerves rose as my eyes scanned the room. The sound of my phone buzzing in my purse interrupted my thoughts. I raced across the room, naked from the waist down, to avoid missing the call.

"Hello?" I answered in such a rush I hadn't looked to see the name on the screen.

"Happy birthday, honey," my mom said, enthusiastically.

Oh yeah, today is my birthday.

"What are you doing today?" I wanted to tell her I was paying homage to her by getting in stirrups and having a doctor look at my vagina, but just before I could speak the door opened.

"I can't talk right now. I'll call you later," I said, hanging up quickly. I was embarrassed I'd been caught with no pants on, talking on the phone. I settled myself on the table. The nurse handed me a small cup of water and a cup with four Ibuprofen tablets inside. "You should take these now, so they'll kick in by the time you're done."

"Cheers," I said, emptying both cups' contents into my mouth.

"Go ahead and lay back. I'll need you to scooch down a little," the doctor instructed. Getting into the right position while in stirrups was somewhat of an art, one I seemed to always struggle with. There was an x-ray machine placed directly above my abdomen and a small monitor allowing me to watch what was going on.

"I am going to insert a catheter into your cervix. You might feel a little pressure," he said. I felt the small rubber tube pushing its way into my uterus. "I'm now injecting iodine to offer contrast on the x-ray. This will show me if your tubes are open and flowing without any blockage." I could see the contrast on the screen, the swirling movement of the fluid hypnotic and calming.

"Those are your fallopian tubes," he said, pointing to what looked like small bolts of lightning. "It looks like the fluid is flowing through both with no issue." I felt relieved to know my tubes were open and my eggs were able to flow through them during ovulation.

This good news came with the stark reminder more testing would be required to eliminate other complications. Selfishly, I'd been hoping James' morphology would be the only hurdle we would have to overcome.

As he removed the catheter, I felt a sharp cramp in my pelvis. I was thankful for the Ibuprofen I'd taken, but the pain continued well into my birthday dinner that evening.

A week later, I had my blood drawn to test my ovarian reserve. This would estimate the number of eggs I released each month. The following day, while sitting at my desk, drafting an email, I looked at my phone to see the fertility clinic calling.

"Do you have a moment?" the nurse asked. "I have your results." Even though I was busy and under a time crunch, this wasn't the type of call I was going to postpone.

I picked up a pen and pad of paper and walked to the conference room for privacy. This room had become all too familiar to me during the last several months. It was the only place I felt I could talk without everyone in my office knowing what was going on with my uterus and James' sperm.

"So, it looks like you are producing a less than average amount of eggs. You fall in the twenty-fifth percentile of egg production for your age." This meant seventy-five percent of women my age were producing more eggs than me. "The good news is you *are* producing eggs, and it only takes one!" This was yet another phrase I grew to resent.

After another week of waiting, we were back in Dr. Hall's office, and it was here he delivered the news we had dreaded but assumed was coming.

"Because of your lower egg count and the abnormal shape of James' sperm, the odds of you getting pregnant naturally are low." His tone remained steady and very matter of fact.

"There is no need to perform any other testing. This complication is enough to warrant assistance," he continued, seemingly hopeful I would be happy to know all testing had concluded.

Disappointment set in, his voice grew muffled in my ears. My eyes filled with tears, and I felt my body slump at the weight of what this meant. Our journey down a road we never expected to travel would have to continue. We would now be faced with options that were not only complicated, but costly. What came in the following moments, as well as months, was more acronyms, probes, and front-row seats to the sperm rodeo.

CHAPTER 3

After being told what our results meant for our chances of getting pregnant naturally, Dr. Hall presented us with two options. Both were complicated in nature and offered different pros and cons.

"IUI, or intrauterine insemination, involves placing sperm directly inside a woman's uterus to help facilitate fertilization," he explained. I made myself comfortable in the blue wingback chair across his desk, knowing we might be there a while. "Some women have a condition called cervical hostility. This is when cervical fluid attacks the sperm as it makes its way into the uterus. The theory around IUI is to bypass this hostile mucus so more sperm can get in."

"Wait," I interrupted, needing to acknowledge the irony of this concept. "My body has been trying to murder James' sperm?" I'd never known my body was trying to kill the very thing it needed to create life.

"Simply put, yes. It seems like a cruel and counterproductive reality, doesn't it?" he said, pausing only a moment before further describing what an IUI entailed. With each new clinical detail, the image of romance faded.

"I will warn you, however, if you don't get pregnant within the first three attempts, I strongly advise you to move on to IVF," he said, then paused to let the information settle. "Because you have a low egg count, I am even less optimistic this method is the best choice at this time."

What did he know?!

"IVF, or in-vitro fertilization, is a bit more invasive," he said, immediately moving to our second option. "The process entails surgically extracting eggs, selecting a single, healthy sperm, and manually combining the two within a glass, which is the meaning of in-vitro." He paused, taking a small sip of water. "The successful combination of the sperm and egg creates an embryo that is either frozen or transferred into the uterus within five to six days via an IUI."

He further explained because the embryo is created and grown outside the body, bypassing its journey through the fallopian tubes, you are considered two weeks pregnant if the transfer is successful.

"Women are born with all the eggs they will ever have. Every month, a number of those eggs sit inside individual follicles, which are sacs filled with fluid, as they grow and mature for ovulation. Your body naturally makes a limited amount of FSH, or follicle-stimulating hormone, which is essentially the food that helps the eggs grow. Ovulation is the result of one egg receiving the majority of the FSH and becoming the dominant egg." He paused again. I frantically wrote notes to ensure I would remember all these details, most of which I was hearing for the first time.

"Once the dominant egg ovulates, all the other eggs that didn't receive enough FSH die, never to be seen again."

I envisioned I was hosting the "Hunger Games" in my ovaries every month. My eggs were the tributes from each district, and the dominant egg was forced to kill all the others to be crowned victor and upgrade its living situation. I laughed silently at the imagery unfolding in my mind.

"IVF offers assistance in the form of daily FSH shots. As a result, more follicles are nourished, allowing more eggs to grow and become viable candidates for fertilization," he said.

He went into specific details about how long shots were administered, how progress was monitored, and what egg extraction entailed. My hand began to cramp. There was so much information to take in, but I knew this was only the tip of the iceberg known as infertility. I was thankful he took the time to lay out in such detail what we faced, but also just wanted him to stop talking.

As he presented the scientific facts about infertility, I became angry it wasn't a topic discussed more openly or with more acceptance. Admitting you needed help procreating wasn't shameful. It didn't imply you were less fit to be a parent or mean you were a failure. Why should anyone feel less adequate or capable because their body produced fewer eggs or questionable swimmers? After all, those things didn't make someone less deserving of a family.

"I think IVF is the best option for the two of you," Dr. Hall said, after presenting all the facts. "But we can certainly try an IUI or two if that is where you would like to start."

I sat in silence, staring out the window at the bright blue sky, forcing James to ask follow-up questions and soak in the answers. I fought back tears, conflicted between knowing this was now my reality and forcing myself to remember how lucky I was to live in a day and age where these options are even possible. I was on a teeter-totter of emotions as I continued to listen. My anger rose only to fall quickly as sadness pushed its way to the top.

Our appointment ended, and James and I walked quietly together to our car. He held my hand and led me to the passenger side, opening and closing the door for me. Neither of us wanted to break the unspoken thoughts undoubtedly swirling in both our minds. This was the first time in years I felt uncomfortable sitting in silence with James.

"Well," I said, being the first to speak. "That was a lot of information. What did you think?" He let out a heavy sigh. I knew he hadn't had enough time to process everything, and I was putting him on the spot.

"Honestly, I feel conflicted," he responded. "I tried paying attention to everything, but each time he said something new I was left wondering how much this all might cost. I know that's not important, but it kept polluting my thoughts."

I'd been so busy taking notes the potential expense hadn't entered my mind. I assumed both IUI and IVF were expensive but didn't know exact figures.

Soon after getting home, I started doing research. I found one cycle of IVF could cost anywhere from $15,000 to $25,000, if not more. IUI's were about $450 per attempt. Although James and I both made a good living and had some money saved, it was hard to look at the cost difference and not feel like there was a clear decision.

I'd been working as a trust manager at a reputable financial institution for nearly eleven years and had recently learned my employer offered financial aid for infertility treatments. This made the burden of an IVF cycle seem much lighter and within our reach. However, I needed to switch to my employer's insurance to qualify, which couldn't happen until the new year, roughly five months away.

We decided to start with an IUI, despite Dr. Hall's concern it might not work.

CHAPTER 4

After making our decision, I was instructed to track my ovulation. I immediately went to the local CVS Pharmacy and found the Clearblue Advanced Digital ovulation test Dr. Hall had recommended. I purchased a few, just to be safe. After several days of waking up and peeing on a plastic stick, I was finally at my peak. I called to let Dr. Hall know.

"You used the *advanced* test?" he asked. I excitedly waved the test in the air as if he would be able to see the smiley face flashing on the screen.

"Yes, you said to use Clearblue Digital. I assume the advanced is better for tracking, right?" I replied.

"One would think so, based on the name," he said in his usual soft monotone. "What you need is the *regular* Clearblue Digital test. That's the one I trust."

There had been no mention of avoiding the advanced test. But due to his opinion of its unreliability, I was told he didn't want to waste our time or money attempting an IUI that month. Hanging up, I was angry, frustrated, and confused. Yet again, we had to wait.

A month later, now mid-August, having stocked up on the Clearblue Digital (non-advanced) tests, I started my tracking again. About nine days into my cycle, I peed on my first stick. No sign of ovulating. It would continue that way for a few days, and I always had some bit of fear. Did I do it at the right time of the day? Should I take another one to be sure? Why is it blinking for so long?

I finally got my first smiley face and was so excited I almost kissed the stick I'd just peed on. I ran into the room to show James, flinging the test around as droplets of urine landed on both of our hands. I didn't even care, that drop was as good as gold. I immediately called the clinic. We were instructed to come in the following day to do our first IUI. We felt a hope we hadn't felt in several months after so much disappointment.

That evening, I lay in bed scrolling through my phone. James had just finished brushing his teeth and stood in our bedroom doorway.

"I have something for you," he said, a boyish grin on his face. "Sort of a good luck charm for tomorrow."

"What is it?" I asked, knowing I wouldn't find out that easily.

"Close your eyes and open your hands," he ordered. I sat up and obliged. Not knowing what to expect, I cupped my hands together as one would when trying to collect rainwater.

"Now you can open," he said, placing a small object in my palm. I took a moment to feel what he'd just given me, thinking I might be able to guess without looking. I opened my eyes and saw a small metal square pin in my hand. A portrait of a smiling family from our favorite cartoon, *Rick and Morty*, appeared in front of me—Mr. Poopy Butthole, his wife, and their child.

Although not a main character and a name that might leave one scratching their head, Mr. Poopy Butthole had come to win our affection, as we empathized with various life struggles we'd seen him face. I looked at the picture and started to cry.

"I can't wait until we have our own Poopy Butthole baby," I said, leaning toward James and pressing my head into his chest.

The following morning, we returned to the familiar waiting room, my good luck charm pinned to my shirt, and checked in. Our IUI experience began with collecting another fresh semen sample from James.

Shortly after arriving, James was called back, a promptness we had not been used to. I got up and followed him after the nurse motioned for me to join. Although not sure what my presence would entail, I was happy to be away from the prying eyes and awkward smiles.

We were led back to a room where another nurse was actively cleaning a large, black leather couch with sanitary wipes. The room was already unappealing, and we laughed at how much dirtier it now felt as we awkwardly stood and watched from the hallway. I could only imagine what that room had seen.

"Jenny, you are welcome to go in with James," the nurse said. "Sometimes the wife likes to, you know...help," she said, gesturing air quotes with her hands. Walking in for the first time, it didn't take much to understand what was meant to take place. In addition to the smell of sanitizer on the freshly cleaned couch, there was a small sink, individual packets of non-spermicidal lube, and a basket with some outdated *Playboy* and *Hustler* magazines.

"I can see they spare no expense for the men," I said, gesturing at the reading material. For all the elaborate testing methods used on women, it seemed the experience for men was much simpler.

The next twenty minutes were more stressful than we anticipated. James had hoped my presence would provide an intimacy and connection this entire process had already taken from us. He thought being together during each step would make a clinical circumstance feel more natural, if possible.

Although a sweet sentiment, I was certain I'd let James have his privacy in the future. Having me in the room added to the anxiety of knowing someone was on the other side of the wall waiting for his sample. Not to mention, it was clear this room was a semen factory, and the next couple was probably already lined up, hand-stamped, waiting to go through the turnstile.

Before the IUI, there was a ninety-minute window for the andrologist to "wash and spin" James' sperm to eliminate some of the problematic ones. We headed to a nearby coffee shop to plug in and catch up on work. Sitting across from one another, feet intertwined under the table, James' phone rang just as he lifted his cup to take a sip.

"I'm at a doctor's appointment right now," he told the caller. "I'll be in the office in a few hours."

"I'd have given you a million dollars to tell whomever that was you just got finished jerking off into a cup," I said, laughing as he hung up. I secretly hoped his phone would ring again and he would take me up on my offer.

We returned to the clinic and were led into a different section we'd not been to before. Wasting no time, I pulled off my jeans and underwear and sat atop the crinkly exam table paper. Flexing my feet, I realized I never knew if I should keep my socks on when told to "undress from the waist down."

An unfamiliar nurse came in, holding a paper in one hand and a catheter and syringe in the other. A small concentration of James' sperm that had just finished a spin cycle could be seen inside. She asked him to verify his name and birthdate were accurately printed on a label affixed to the tube. It became clear to me this process required an unwavering amount of trust; no other proof needed.

With my feet now in stirrups, I felt much like a turkey about to be basted on Thanksgiving. Once the catheter was put into place, she counted to three and pushed the small amount of opaque fluid into my uterus and held up the empty syringe as proof. I was tilted back on the table and instructed to lie with my legs elevated for about ten minutes.

That is the romantic story of how James and I would hopefully conceive our first child. We were both hit with a wave of emotions thinking of everything that had led us to this magical moment. We held hands and talked about how excited we were and how hard it was going to be to wait fourteen excruciating days before knowing the results. I felt a sense of relief believing this would be the end of our fertility struggle.

Our ten-minute timer went off, I got dressed and made sure the Poopy Butthole family was still securely attached to my shirt. We each headed to work, moving on with our day knowing everything was the same, except now, I carried precious cargo.

Over the next two weeks, I found it difficult to find ways of distracting myself while waiting. I kept myself busy with work and social engagements, but the anticipation and hope were always at the forefront of my thoughts. Although I'd come to know the exact date and time, within an hour, my period would start, I couldn't stand the suspense of waiting for the day to arrive. I took two early detection pregnancy tests and was disappointed to see *negative* flash on the screen.

The day I expected to start my period finally arrived. I sat at work in a padded leather chair in the back corner of the conference room, waiting for my fifteen colleagues to shuffle in. I'd become accustomed, in these bi-weekly meetings, to arrive a few minutes early to ensure I wouldn't end up with one of the broken chairs everyone avoided.

The room eventually quieted as the lights dimmed and I leaned back in my chair. I felt a familiar sensation, one I realized I'd not been prepared for. I looked at the clock. *Shit, this can't be happening, not now.* I abruptly stood and made my way to the front of the room, trying not to bump into anyone or cause a scene. I tried to prevent any evidence from making itself known by carefully waddling my way toward the bathroom.

There it was. The harsh realization our IUI had not worked. I felt all the hope drain from my body, literally and figuratively, as if to also be flushed down the toilet. A sudden bout of nausea came over me. I sat in the stall, pants around my knees, a wad of toilet paper in my hand, and tried to muffle my sobs. The echo in the bathroom carried, and I didn't want to have to explain to anyone what had just happened. I wiped away my tears. *I don't even have a tampon with me.* I realized I hadn't brought one to the bathroom, and I knew I didn't have one in my purse. The dispenser in the bathroom was useless. I'd wasted several quarters trying to avoid the walk of shame back to my desk. I had to not only make that walk, but approach someone to ask for help.

A few coworkers knew about our recent IUI, but I didn't feel prepared to face them and reveal my body had failed me. I also had to decide if my circumstance needed immediate attention or if I could take a few moments to privately call James. Either way, I knew there would be a lot of crying involved. I stuffed my underwear with toilet paper, pulled up my pants, and left the bathroom to call James.

"Babe," I said, my somber tone a stark contrast to his joyful one, "it didn't work." As expected, I started crying the moment the words came out of my mouth. I struggled to keep my composure enough to even finish the sentence. It felt reminiscent of childhood when I got hurt on the playground. I was fine until I saw my mom, when I'd completely break down while telling her what had happened.

James took a moment to respond. The silence, although momentary, was deafening.

"Fuck," he said. "Jen, I'm so sorry. For you, for us. Are you okay?" I was not able to respond, my emotions continued to overwhelm me. "Babe, it's going to be okay. I promise." His tone was calm and compassionate, but his disappointment was palpable. "We knew the first one might not work, and we can do it again next month."

I left work early, immediately finding the comfort of my bed when I got home. I wanted to sleep away my pain. I woke up before James got home from work and poured myself a rather sizable glass of red wine. I sat on the couch with my loyal companion: Gus, the five-year-old Corgi James had given me for Christmas in 2013.

I sipped my wine and let tears drop from my eyes. Gus always seemed to know when I cried. He looked at me as I gently stroked his back. He was the only dog I'd ever known to hold a gaze, never being first to blink. He licked the tears rolling down my face, something he always did when I cried. I realized at that moment I was already a mom.

In mid-September, we prepared for our second IUI. It started to feel like Groundhog Day as the entire cycle started over again. Wake up, pee on the stick, wait for a smiley face, repeat. The night before IUI number two, James presented me with a small, wrapped box.

I tore open the paper revealing a small, vinyl, cowboy figurine, dressed in a hat, cowhide chaps, a red bandana, and little spurs on his boots. Going along with the *Rick and Morty* theme of my first good luck charm, Western Morty looked at me from inside the clear plastic packaging.

"I thought this was funny because he's a cowboy," James said. "You know, to wrangle up the sperm in the sperm rodeo," he added, realizing I'd not immediately made the connection.

"Oh my God," I exclaimed, "my own sperm rodeo Morty!" I couldn't wait to take him along with my pin to our appointment the next day.

The second IUI was much like the first. This time, I didn't accompany James to the collection room, but rather, remained in the waiting room. He returned faster this time, leading me to believe he'd overcome the stage fright he previously experienced. During the ninety-minute wait, James went to the coffee shop to work, and I went to the gym. It felt natural to work up a bit of a sweat if I was about to possibly become pregnant.

"All set!" another new nurse said, after emptying the contents of the syringe into my uterus. "Now, lay back for ten minutes and you are free to go. I also recommend you go home and have as much sex as you can in the next forty-eight hours." These were instructions we hadn't received before but obliged as best we could over the next two days. If I got pregnant, we could still claim we'd had our baby naturally as it would be impossible to tell if we'd conceived at the IUI or during intercourse.

We did everything we were supposed to do over the next fourteen days. However, after more waiting came more disappointment—my period. Again, met with tears and anger, I began to resent my body for betraying me over and over. I was growing bitter about the entire experience. And to make matters worse on my emotional fragility, I kept seeing Facebook notifications from friends announcing happy news they were expecting. I was being invited to baby showers left and right.

I felt I was being forced to be happy for others while I slowly crumbled on the inside. It was hard to balance being happy for and celebrating my friends while simultaneously experiencing jealousy and anger about my situation. Although I couldn't know what their journey had looked like to get pregnant, I felt envious due to my own struggle. Why couldn't that be me?

In October and November, we attempted two more IUIs. For attempt three, James wore the jersey of his favorite Utah Jazz basketball player, Bryon Russell, who was number three. However, I was met with yet another period. We decided to try a fourth and final IUI in November. If not successful, we would take a much-needed break before moving on to IVF at the beginning of the year, when I would start receiving the fertility benefit from my employer. Feeling overly frustrated and exhausted, we knew we were going to need more than luck for our last IUI, and this time, there was no good luck charm.

While waiting for the results of our final attempt, we traveled to Indiana to visit my extended family. My aunt had recently been diagnosed with terminal stage IV pancreatic cancer. For those few days, I didn't think about pregnancy or babies, but rather about how fragile and fleeting life can be. Regardless of my difficulty getting pregnant, life, as well as death, was happening all around us. I focused on building joyful memories of times spent with family and sorrowful moments of saying goodbye. By the time we got home, I realized I was two days late.

I was filled with an excitement and nervousness only one waiting for the results of a pregnancy test can feel. As two more days came and went, so did my usual desire to immediately take a test. If our fourth IUI had worked and I was pregnant, I could wait a few more days to ensure I trusted the results. If I wasn't pregnant, I wanted to at least hold on to this morsel of hope, or delusion, for a few more days.

I started convincing myself I was experiencing the first signs of pregnancy. I was tired, bloated, and nauseous. All signs pointed to good news. Except, as I'd experienced hundreds of times before with PMS, I also felt moody, my boobs were sore, and I was cramping.

Holding on to hope is a tricky thing. On one hand, it allows you to succumb to your deepest and most delicate vulnerabilities. It allows you to see the good in a situation no matter how easy it can be to recognize the bad. On the other hand, it can give you a false sense of security that tosses your vulnerability to the wind and knocks you on your ass. I was tired of holding on to hope only to find myself on the ground once again, continually trying to convince myself next time would be different.

On day five of my missed period, I finally took a pregnancy test, certain the result would be what I'd longed to see. How can one tiny little stick cause so much happiness or so much heartache? I would have done anything just to feel the relief and excitement of knowing my body could create a life.

Another negative showed in front of me. *This couldn't be right.* I took a second test. Negative. I called my doctor and scheduled a blood test for the following day. However, that evening my period was ever so present, and yet again, grief knocked me on my ass. Although we had only done this IUI as somewhat a formality, we still felt devastated.

A few days later, we gathered with James' family to celebrate Thanksgiving. Even though we'd suffered a lot of heartache and sadness, we still had so much to be thankful for. Full of turkey and more wine than I'd intended, I went into my sisters-in-law's room to lay down.

The bed was soft and the room dark, except for a small amount of light visible through a gap in the curtains. I heard laughter coming from downstairs, but I began to tear up thinking how difficult the last few months had been. Curled in the fetal position, I realized I could no longer hold in the sobs I fought to contain. I was glad no one could see me as a mixture of tears and snot streamed down my face and onto my sister-in-law's pillow.

Moments later, I heard the bedroom door slowly creak open. Light crept across the floor and onto the wall, disappearing as the door clicked shut. I sniffled softly as footsteps approached the bed and my body shifted at the weight of someone climbing onto the mattress to join me. I assumed the person curling behind and wrapping their arms around me was James.

"Everything is going to be okay," I heard, softly whispered in my ear. A dainty hand brushed away the hair sticking to my face. I realized it wasn't James, but his mom. She was one of only a few people who'd known about our IUI attempts. We had shared this information with her, not only because of our close relationship but because she'd also gone through IUIs to conceive her children.

While working as a rehabilitation nurse in the 1980s, she had a patient who'd become paralyzed after a motorcycle accident. While caring for this man, a relationship formed, and they were eventually married. Due to his injuries however, he was no longer able to have children of his own. Naturally, they wanted a family together and began researching their options, deciding on anonymous sperm donation. They began working through a local andrology clinic and soon after, chose a donor.

She had an IUI, this being the common method used to conceive with sperm donation, and became pregnant with James' sister. Two years later, after eight IUI attempts, she was able to get pregnant with James. Four IUI attempts had taken their toll on me physically and emotionally. How she went through eight was completely unfathomable to me.

"I'm so scared," I said, as she continued stroking my hair. "What if I can't get pregnant? What if I can't give James a child?" All the while, she remained silent and held me. I didn't need her to answer any of my questions nor did I expect she'd have the right thing to say. I hadn't known how much I needed her at that moment.

Lying there with me, I felt her softly crying as she held me tighter. It was comforting to know James and I weren't alone, that others had been or were going down the same path. It was at this moment I knew the only way I could regain control of my journey was to be as open and vulnerable with others about everything we would go through moving forward.

With no more IUIs for the rest of the year, we were able to take a symbolic breath of fresh air. There were no ovulation tests, no timers for sex, and no awkward fertility clinic visits. We ended 2018 with clear minds and a renewed resolve to continue forward in the new year.

CHAPTER 5

January 2019 eventually arrived, and with it, our next step began—a step I'd been dreading because of my lifetime hatred of needles.

I wasn't looking forward to the two weeks' worth of daily hormone injections. I was now entering a fertility phase that although surprisingly common, put James and me into an exclusive club. We met with a nurse to learn how to measure and administer the medication.

"*THAT* is the needle we have to use?" I asked, my heart racing as I watched her unwrap a syringe. "It looks like a penne noodle!"

"No, don't worry, this is just the needle used to draw out the fluid," she said, reassuringly. "This is the needle you'll use." She held up a much smaller and thinner needle, leading me to stop clenching every muscle in my body.

On January 18, I had blood drawn to measure my hormone levels. It was the first of many needle pricks to come. We were sent home with syringes, alcohol wipes, vials of Gonal F and Menopur (both containing FSH), and a red needle receptacle.

The next day between dinner and bedtime, the time we were instructed to administer my shots every day, we braved our new adventure together.

"Are you recording?" I asked. I'd wanted to document our journey so one day we'd be able to share the videos and memories with our child.

"Yep!" James answered, holding his phone. I began drawing saline out of the first vial before mixing it with the medication in the second vial. I looked at the piece of paper I'd attempted to scribble notes on days before.

"Dang it," I said, looking at the different vials sitting on our granite countertop in front of me. "I think I did what I wasn't supposed to. I was only supposed to mix one mL of fluid and I did two." I nervously contemplated discarding the fluid I'd incorrectly mixed but refrained. After all, this stuff wasn't cheap. "Oh well, it's just saline. Just means there will be more fluid going in my body."

After measuring, mixing, and swapping out needles, James knelt on the kitchen floor. I lifted my shirt, and he cleaned a section of skin to the left of my belly button with an alcohol wipe.

"It will be just fine," he said, rising to give me a kiss. I took a deep breath in and stared at the needle in his hand as he plunged it into the clump of skin I pinched tightly between my fingers. The fluid slowly entered my body with a late-onset burning sensation. I tapped my foot in pain as he finished.

"Good job, good job!" he said, rubbing my leg.

"Oh, next time we won't use as much liquid!" I said, nervously laughing away the pain. I released my grip and could see white finger marks on my belly. He picked up the second syringe, asking if we should switch to another spot.

"No, you didn't clean the other side, just do it here," I said, pointing to the same sanitized area. The second injection didn't go as smoothly. The needle bounced off my skin, causing my jaw to tighten as I tried not to scream. After loosening my grasp, James made another attempt, which was successful. In sync we let out groans of discomfort followed by laughs of relief. Day one of fourteen was complete.

Over the next week, the shots became easier to administer, but I was beginning to feel the effects of the hormones. Tiny red dots marked my stomach with each new prick, and it was normal to look down and see the discolored bruises decorating my abdomen. I felt bloated and much like a pin cushion. I could only hope the medication was helping my body create enough eggs to make this experience worth it.

After our fourth evening of shots, I thought back to Thanksgiving and the experience I'd had with James' mom. I remembered the promise I'd made about being open and vulnerable about our journey. That evening, I took to Facebook to post pictures and videos of our first few days of IVF as well as recap what we had gone through over the last fifteen months.

I was humbled by the support I received and shocked at the number of people who reached out to tell me of their own experiences with infertility. I couldn't believe how many friends had struggled to get pregnant. My heart ached for them, knowing they'd suffered in silence through multiple failed IUI attempts or rounds of IVF. I was again angry infertility wasn't talked about more openly as it was apparent this struggle was not only real, but also more common than I could have ever imagined.

I was determined to normalize discussions around infertility and felt empowered by my newfound support. I wanted to share that I was learning to not be ashamed of my body, but rather thankful I had options and resources to help me get through it.

On day eight, we introduced a third medication that would stop my body from ovulating naturally. Because the purpose of IVF is to extract eggs while they are still in the ovaries, it is imperative ovulation doesn't occur.

We happened to be having dinner at a friend's house to celebrate the news they were expecting. The irony was not lost on us. We went into a small half-bathroom for privacy. Part of me wanted to pull out all the syringes right in the middle of the appetizers and drinks. If I had to go through this, why couldn't everyone sit and watch how awful it was and feel bad for me?

The needle for this injection was thicker than the others. My heart started pounding at the thought of poking a larger hole in my already raw skin. I was also nervous about how my body might react to an unfamiliar medication. In this half-bathroom, barely big enough for the two of us, James kneeled between the toilet and sink and held my hand. It was almost as romantic as when he got on one knee in Central Park and asked me to be his wife.

"You're going to do just great," he said softly, not breaking his gaze. "You've been so strong through all this, and you can get through more." The sound of our friends talking cheerfully in the background was a stark contrast to the dread I felt in the bathroom.

The following day, we had another blood draw and ultrasound to assess my progress. Each month, the clinic grouped all the IVF patients into a "batch" and rotated which doctor took all the cases. This helped to align and control the schedule for monitoring and egg extraction. Because of my cycle's timing, we were put in a batch with Dr. Smith, whom we'd met during a previous encounter at the clinic.

"Good morning," he said, looking at my chart, rather than at James and me. "I am Dr. Smith. Looks like we're here to check your ovaries for follicles today?" He clearly hadn't remembered us. *You saw my ovaries three weeks ago, how do you not recognize me?* I looked at James, who rolled his eyes. I could tell he was also annoyed at the lackluster greeting.

Dr. Smith began the ultrasound and counted out loud the number of follicles he could see, measured them, and mumbled to his nurse a few times. He appeared to be nearing the end of the exam when something on the screen caught his eye. He tilted his head back and forth while trying to identify an image he saw on my ovary.

"It looks kind of fuzzy," he described, pressing his index finger directly on the screen. "I can't be certain, but my guess is it's a fibroid," he said, adding a fibroid is a common non-cancerous cyst that can grow large enough to create fertility problems. "Let's keep an eye on it to make sure it doesn't get too big. Unfortunately the only treatment is surgery. We'll take another look in two days." Although he hadn't seemed too concerned, I wondered if I should be, considering my family's medical history.

When I was a sophomore in high school, my mom was diagnosed with breast cancer at the age of fifty-three. She went through several rounds of chemotherapy and radiation, followed by a double mastectomy. The youngest of four kids, I was the only child living at home during this time, as all my siblings had gone off to college. I was scared to know my mom had a life-threatening disease, but I viewed her as invincible and didn't allow myself to imagine the worst. She'd found it early, and her chemo didn't result in hair loss, so I assumed she was in a better spot than most. Her treatment was successful, and she went into remission, but a year later, she was diagnosed with ovarian cancer. This time, her treatment was more intense.

One night, between her first and second infusions, we sat and watched TV in her room, the only thing she had energy to do. I noticed her focus was not on the TV and watched as her hand lifted toward her head. She pulled out a large chunk of hair and examined it before setting it in her lap. She immediately reached up and pulled out more, as if testing to see if the first time was a fluke. An even larger chunk remained between her tightly-pressed fingers as she completed a second examination. She repeated this motion a few more times, not realizing I was watching.

"Mom, stop!" I cried, grabbing her wrist firmly as if I was the parent now scolding my child. She looked at me, no discernable expression present on her face, and reached for another tug.

"It's kind of fun," she said, her tone void of emotion. "Here, you try." Wanting to be supportive in a moment I could only imagine was difficult, I hesitantly reached over and pulled. We both looked at the hair in my hand before adding it to the pile in her lap. The next day, I got home from school to find she'd gone to the neighbor's house and shaved her head.

After my mom beat cancer for a second time, she went through a clinical study that offered free genetic testing. Her results came back indicating she was positive for BRCA 1 mutation. BRCA is an abbreviation for a 'BReast CAncer' gene, and there are two different forms of the gene, 1 and 2 (meaning they are found on different chromosomes).

Every human has BRCA 1 and BRCA 2 genes they receive from both parents. These genes produce proteins that help repair damaged DNA, and despite what their names might suggest, they do not cause breast cancer, but rather, suppress the growth of cancer cells or tumors. Sometimes however, these genes don't work properly, which, in turn, classifies them as mutated. This mutation can lead to increased risks of various cancers, mostly breast and ovarian, and it had likely caused my mother's illness.

I decided to get tested for the gene mutation when I was nineteen years old and was similarly positive. Although not a guarantee, it did mean my risk for having ovarian cancer was close to forty-four percent and nearly seventy-two percent for breast cancer. I used this knowledge to be proactive at a young age in both yearly pap tests as well as mammograms.

My fertility doctors were aware of my BRCA 1 mutation and informed me of my potential risks moving forward with IVF. This included the possibility of passing the genetic mutation to my child. They also explained how introducing hormones into my body, via daily shots, could add to my already higher risk of breast and ovarian cancer.

Although the idea of passing the BRCA 1 mutation on to my future children did give me pause, I felt confident it was something we could navigate. Having found out myself, at an early age, I'd been diligent in my screenings and believed in doing so, I'd have a better chance of early detection. I was also confident medical advancements would continue to be made over the course of my life, as well as my children's lives, to help identify and monitor potential risks. And of course, it was also possible the mutation wouldn't be passed down at all.

We returned to the clinic for another follicle monitoring appointment two days later, this time joined by Dr. Hall. The "fuzzy" images still appeared on my scan but didn't seem to be getting worse.

"I suppose they could be fibroids, but I am also not certain," Dr. Hall said, looking at the monitor. I could tell it weighed on him not to have an answer. We had one more appointment the following day to check my follicles before determining the plan for my egg retrieval. I figured if nothing else, they would get a better view during my surgery.

Tuesday morning, I was back on the table receiving what I hoped would be our final progress assessment. The nurse dimmed the fluorescent lights to a warm shade. The room suddenly felt more like a spa, and I expected to hear Enya songs playing in the background. I felt relaxed and comfortable while watching the nurse prepare for my ultrasound. A machine next to me blew warm air while softly humming, causing my eyelids to feel heavy. Both doctors entered the room, and I felt James' grasp tighten on my shoulder.

"I reviewed your images again last night," Dr. Hall said. He'd finished the exam and turned the lights back on. "I felt unsettled. So, I decided to reach out to a former colleague of mine. She is a gynecological oncologist." The word *oncologist* brought an immediate stab of pain in my stomach. "I asked for her thoughts, and she recommended you come in and see her as soon as possible after your egg retrieval."

Although relieved we could still proceed with the extraction, I was in shock at his recommendation. I squeezed James' hand. I'd hoped to see the usual calm on his face, but instead, his brows furrowed with concern. Both of us were still adjusting to the blaring lights that only moments ago had made us feel at ease.

"Until you see her and we have more clarity, I'm not sure I feel comfortable completing a transfer on day five," he said. I felt my body temperature begin to rise and pulled at my shirt's neckline. The room seemed to suddenly be a lot smaller. James moved his hand to the small of my back while we both absorbed what this meant. I no longer felt like I was in a spa, but in a prison cell for a crime I didn't commit. The last thing James and I wanted was to wait any longer. We'd expected to know within two weeks whether or not we were going to have a baby. Freezing and thawing embryos could add six to nine weeks to the already lengthy process.

I didn't have any other choice but to agree. Leaving the clinic James asked how I felt. I didn't have words to express anything but anger. I was pissed at my body and feared what this meant.

"I don't feel like talking right now," I said. I quickly got into my car and drove away, sobbing the entire thirty-minute drive to work. Fear took over, and I began to think of all the worst-case scenarios. Was I sick? Was I going to die? Was I even going to be able to have a baby? These thoughts ran through my mind as I tried to navigate my way safely through the traffic buzzing around me.

Upon parking my car at work, I realized I hadn't called the oncologist to make an appointment because I'd been too busy falling apart. I dug through my purse for the number Dr. Hall had given me and quickly dialed it.

"I have an egg retrieval this Thursday, and if there is still a chance to do a fresh transfer next Tuesday, I *have* to see the doctor on Friday or Monday," I told the nurse on the other end of the line.

"Unfortunately, she doesn't have any openings on Friday, and she's not in the office on Monday," she told me. I sat in silence, not sure what to say, and began to cry.

"Please," I begged. "Is there *anything* you can do for me? I need to see her on Friday. You don't understand." I blubbered. I wasn't even contemplating the urgency to know if something was wrong with my ovaries.

"I understand and am so sorry you are going through this," she said, her tone kind and empathetic. "Let me see what I can do to get you in on Friday." She promised to call me back. Looking in the mirror, I realized in addition to adding tampons to my purse, I needed to start packing extra makeup as these emotional breakdowns began happening more frequently.

An hour later, the nurse called to tell me she'd gotten me on the schedule at 7:45 Friday morning. I felt like Samantha on *Sex and the City* when she'd been able to get an appointment with an oncologist, whose schedule was completely booked, by telling the receptionist she was dating a movie star. I wasn't dating anyone famous and only got the appointment because I sobbed on the phone, but I still felt beyond relieved. Now I could go about my day hoping there might still be a window for a fruitful end to our IVF journey.

CHAPTER 6

T hursday, January 31, James and I drove to the fertility clinic for my egg retrieval. Wednesday had been the first in fourteen days James didn't need to administer any shots. Maybe it was everything we'd gone through in the last six months or because I was immensely uncomfortable, bloated, and sore, but it felt like we'd been on this IVF journey far longer than two weeks.

I couldn't wait to see how the difficulties we'd endured would pay off, and I would finally get to use my coupons. I saw a light shining on our past disappointments, making them momentarily seem miles away. James and I proved, yet again, that we could overcome any trial we faced and come out better on the other side.

The frigid January cold made me thankful for seat-warmers in the car. Dressed in my comfiest clothes, I'd remembered to pin the Poopy Butthole family to my shirt, and Sperm Rodeo Morty was nestled in my purse. Alongside him was a new and final good luck charm James had given me the night before.

Avid fans of *Game of Thrones*, we'd spent a ridiculous amount of time rewatching the series. Its final season, 2019, was the biggest year for the show. After finishing an episode, James announced he had one more good luck charm for me. I closed my eyes and instinctively held out my hands. *How sad. This is probably the last good luck charm I will get.*

I opened my eyes to see two cream-colored drawstring bags with the *Game of Thrones* logo printed on the outside. I set one on the table with a loud thud and untied the impossible knot I'd come to anticipate from James. I pulled out a beautiful, dark green resin-carved dragon egg. It was heavy in my hands, much like my ovary felt inside my body. I opened the second bag and found a similar egg inside, but this one was red. They were miniature replicas of the dragon eggs gifted to Daenerys Targaryen that would later hatch, making her the "Mother of Dragons."

"I know there are three dragons in the show," James said as my gaze shifted to look for another egg to complete the set, "but I only got two because you only have two ovaries." He paused. "And mostly because they were expensive, and I couldn't justify buying all three!" I laughed and placed the eggs in my purse alongside my other good luck charms.

We arrived at the clinic and were led back to the surgical section, another part of the building we'd not seen before. Behind a thin curtain, James sat with me until he was summoned back to provide yet another semen sample.

This sample would be a little different. Rather than "wash and spin" James' sperm, the andrologist would individually wrangle the best ones to later be injected, via a thin needle, into any of the viable eggs retrieved. Based on my ultrasounds and follicle measurements from days prior, it appeared there were ten maturing follicles between both ovaries.

A friendly nurse, wearing bright pink glasses, led me to the operating room where I made myself comfortable. I was given a warm blanket as the nurse pierced my vein with an IV. Both of my doctors entered the room. "I was able to make an appointment with the oncologist for tomorrow," I told Dr. Hall, who had come to wish me luck.

"I should have some answers afterward, and hopefully we can still do a fresh transfer on Tuesday!" I held my crossed fingers in the air.

"I am glad to hear you got in, and I will keep my fingers crossed as well." He smiled and closed the door behind him. I felt surprisingly touched that he'd taken the time to come in and wish me well.

"While you are anesthetized, I'll use the ultrasound to guide me to your vaginal wall," Dr. Smith said, holding a wand I'd become familiar with. "I'll use a needle to puncture your ovary and suction out any eggs we aspirate from your follicles. Do you have any questions?" I was tired, scared, and about to have the inside of my vagina punctured. There was nothing more I needed to hear. I shook my head and was happy I didn't have to be awake.

The anesthesiologist told me he was about to inject the medications. "I like to try to fight them," I said aloud, knowing I would never win. "Good luuuuuuuu..." Forty minutes later, I awoke, James at my bedside.

"Everything went well," Dr. Smith said, pulling the curtain to the side and entering the space. "We were able to retrieve three eggs which are in the lab being fertilized as we speak."

"Only three?" I asked. I felt gutted. "I thought there were ten on my ultrasound." This number couldn't be right.

"You had ten maturing follicles, but when we aspirated them, only three eggs were found. The other follicles were empty." He glanced at both of us, allowing time to answer any questions we might have. I felt a sudden cramp in my abdomen and couldn't tell if it was the aftermath of my ovaries being pierced or disappointment about my results. Either way, the pain lingered for the rest of the day.

Each day, the embryologist would check to determine if our embryos were progressing at the appropriate rate. An embryo could be monitored for five days to six days before needing to either be frozen or freshly transferred. Limits in modern fertility technology only permit embryos to live outside of a uterus for up to six days, after which they become unviable.

We would receive updates, with the ultimate hope being that after my appointment with the oncologist, we would get the clear to continue with a fresh transfer and have a healthy, viable embryo to use.

Additionally, if there was still a chance a fresh transfer was in our future, I would have to begin a new daily injection of progesterone, to help thicken and prepare the uterine lining. This shot had to be done intramuscularly, which meant it wouldn't be in my stomach. Because it had to be done in a much meatier spot, my butt, the clinic had drawn two big black circles on either cheek indicating the target area inside where James was to aim.

The day after my retrieval, I lay on the couch as James came face to face with my ass cheek prior to heading to my oncology appointment. I iced the injection site for a few moments in preparation to receive the shot. Yet again, this needle was bigger than all the rest. I could feel James shaking as he tried to empty the syringe into my now numb ass. Being mixed with oil rather than saline, the fluid was thicker and had a harder time flowing into my muscle.

After the injection was done, I stuffed the ice pack in my underwear, and we made our way to the oncology office. When we arrived, the nurse who helped get me this appointment led us to the exam room, took my vitals, and told us the doctor would be in to see us shortly. Knowing this appointment had been made as a kindness to me, I was more than happy to wait.

A few moments after arriving, I received a phone call from the fertility clinic. I recognized the embryologist's voice on the other end. "I am calling to let you know we were able to successfully fertilize two of the three eggs we retrieved," he said. A sigh of relief exited my body. "Unfortunately, one of the eggs just wasn't mature enough and didn't fertilize. We will keep an eye on the remaining two embryos and give you a call on Sunday with an update." This wasn't exactly what we'd hoped to hear but were glad to know that at this point IVF hadn't been a total waste.

A small knock was followed by the doctor entering the room. She wore a long, white lab coat, her name neatly embroidered in cursive font across the left side. She reached out and said, "Hi, I am Dr. Zempolich." I shook her hand and after a bit of small talk, she opened my chart.

She'd reviewed the images Dr. Hall sent over and hadn't been able to make a conclusive diagnosis. I found my sweet spot in the stirrups, and she completed a very short exam. Unfortunately, I was still too swollen from my retrieval, making it impossible for her to see or feel anything that could further her knowledge of what was going on.

"I am going to order you a CT scan," she said, tossing her used gloves in the trash can. "I think it'll be a better way for me to see what's going on." I'd never had a CT scan and didn't know what to expect. "If you can get the scan done today, I'll review the results and call you this weekend. I know you're eager to do a fresh transfer next week." We were able to get an appointment an hour later.

Upon arriving at the hospital, I changed into another gown and had another IV inserted into my bruised vein. The nurse prepared a bottle of Crystal Light lemonade mixed with an oral contrast fluid, instructing me to drink in twenty-minute increments until it was gone. Cold and half-naked, I plugged my nose with every gulp and imagined I was on a beach with a margarita in my hand. After ninety minutes and a few trips to the bathroom to empty my overfilled bladder, I was lying on a table encircled by a large donut-shaped machine.

"I'll take a few images, inject iodine into your IV, then take a few additional images. Have you ever had this dye before?" he asked. I shook my head. "For about thirty seconds you'll feel your body get warm. Most people describe the sensation as feeling like you just wet yourself."

The lights in the room dimmed, a pattern I noticed with these intimidating procedures. The table began to move into the center of the donut. A recording instructed me to hold my breath, followed by instructing me to breathe normally. The table moved in and out a few times, and I continued to follow the commands.

"I'm injecting the dye now. It takes about thirty seconds," the nurse said over a speaker. He was in the next room watching through a window.

The feeling of warmth started in my throat, making me feel a bit nauseous and leaving an awful taste in my mouth. It slowly worked its way through my body. *Oh no, did I just pee?* About a minute later, the table returned to the starting position, and I heard the door of the control room open and close. The nurse helped me to my feet, revealing I hadn't peed myself.

That evening, still feeling beaten and bruised from the events of the last few days, I mustered what small bit of energy I could find and attended a rehearsal dinner for a good friend who'd asked me to be a bridesmaid. Although a necessary distraction, I couldn't completely prevent my thoughts from wandering to my CT scan earlier in the day. I wasn't sure when I would hear back from Dr. Zempolich but knew it probably wouldn't be that evening.

The following day I was faced with similar distractions while the bridal party got ready for the day, including makeup, hair, and mimosas. I did my best to focus on the wedding, which seemed easier with each additional Fireball shot and loud, blaring music, accompanied by singing and dancing. However, every time I found myself alone in the bathroom was another story. The silence and loneliness brought with it a wave of fear I wasn't ready to acknowledge. It was in these moments I allowed myself to admit for the first time I was scared I might be sick.

Sunday morning we received another call from the clinic. "I'm just calling to let you know one of your embryos isn't progressing as much as we'd like to see, but we'll continue to watch it. The other one is looking good so far," the embryologist said. All we could do was hope our two remaining embryos would keep fighting.

First thing Monday morning, after not hearing from Dr. Zempolich over the weekend, I was able to reach her. "The images weren't as clear as I'd hoped," she said. "I think it's a combination of you still being swollen from your retrieval and the possibility there is something going on."

"What does that mean?" I asked. "Am I not able to do a fresh transfer tomorrow? Should I be more concerned?" *Does she not know how important this is to me?* Panic set in.

"I think it would be best for us to go in laparoscopically and look. We can also take a biopsy at the same time." She paused, giving me a moment to process her words. "I wouldn't recommend continuing with a transfer tomorrow. In fact, I have time on Wednesday to get you in for this procedure." We finished speaking, and I was promptly scheduled to be at the hospital two days later.

I hung up the phone feeling defeated. On one hand, I was thankful for the precautions and amount of care I received, but on the other, I felt this decision had been made for me and was angry I seemed to have no say in the matter. Balancing that kind of emotion was difficult, not to mention it was becoming a more regular requirement.

Tuesday morning we received another update. This time, the news wasn't as promising. "Unfortunately, one of them stopped progressing and isn't viable," the embryologist said, his tone apologetic and remorseful. "The other embryo is still not fully hatched, meaning at this point, it isn't fully viable either. We can only watch it for one more day, but if it doesn't progress we won't be able to freeze that one either. I will call you first thing tomorrow to let you know what happens."

It felt like blow after blow, and I was again left to wonder what I'd done in my life to be the recipient of such shitty news. James looked at me, and all I could do was shrug my shoulders. I'd become numb to hearing negative news, and there wasn't much else I could do but move on with my day and hope for the best. I didn't want James to see the heartache I felt and did what I could to appear strong.

CHAPTER 7

Wednesday morning we woke early and made the fifteen-minute drive to the hospital for a seven o'clock check-in time. The garage door opened, revealing it had heavily snowed the night before and didn't appear to be letting up.

"Shit, we are going to be late!" I said. The snow plows hadn't made their rounds in our neighborhood. It felt like an electric shock. My nervousness around what the day held was replaced by panic we wouldn't make it to the hospital on time.

Being the hour it was, I assumed we would be able to avoid the morning rush of people making their way to work. An eeriness blanketed the streets, much like the snow, sitting in a somber, sleepy silence only interrupted by the windshield wipers swooshing.

Entering the freeway, a different scene played out in front of us. Red taillights could be seen in rows as cars inched forward at a snail's pace. Roughly five inches of fresh snow covered the road, and drivers were left to make their own lanes. Having no other route to take, we forged ahead. We slowly passed cars and trucks that had slid off the road, some of which were facing the opposite direction. *Could this be a bad omen?* My hands were clenched in fists, hoping James wouldn't hit a patch of ice and send us to the same fate.

After forty-five stressful minutes on the road, we arrived safely at the hospital. Rushing to the check-in desk, I noticed two familiar faces, sitting in the otherwise empty waiting area. James' parents, who lived even further away from the hospital than we did, smiled back at me. They'd made the long and dangerous journey to wish me luck.

"You guys are crazy!" I said, struggling to speak through a sudden lump in my throat. "What are you doing here? I can't believe you drove in this weather to be here!" I hugged them both and felt a sudden relief and comfort.

"I'm so sorry we are late," I said to the nurse checking me in. "We had no idea it snowed so much. It was insane out there."

"It's alright. In fact, your doctor isn't here yet. She's snowed in and trying to get out of her driveway. She'll be at least an hour late." I half expected her to hand me a coupon for the delay.

We sat quietly in the waiting area until the sound of my phone ringing interrupted the silence. The name of the fertility clinic flashed on the screen. I'd not expected to hear from them this early, but immediately jumped out of my seat and motioned James to follow me to a different spot. "Hello?" I answered, putting the call on speaker.

"Hi, Jennifer. I'm calling to give you the final update on your embryo." I couldn't tell if his tone was positive or negative, but then he exclaimed, "It looks like your little fighter hatched and is ready to be frozen! I had to call you right away because I'm so excited about this news. I even took a picture and sent it in an email."

James and I embraced. "Oh my God, it worked!" I said, breathing a sigh of relief. Our IVF had resulted in a healthy, viable cocktail of our DNA that would hopefully someday become our baby. Tears filled my eyes to hear such wonderful news at a time when other uncertainties loomed. We had this little embryo, we immediately started calling EmbryLowe, that would go into a deep freeze and wake up ready to journey into my uterus when I was cleared to get pregnant. No amount of pain or discomfort I'd felt in the last few weeks and months could take away the joy I felt in that moment. Science was an incredible thing and aided in giving us such a remarkable gift.

Soon after hanging up, I was called back into my pre-op room and was greeted by various nurses. "Would you like a warm blanket?" they asked. *Hell, yes I would.* James began to tease me for continuing to accept a new warm blanket every single time, the count now being around a dozen. It became a joke that I could never turn one down.

After digging out of her snowy driveway, Dr. Zempolich arrived and was ready to begin. Now flat on my back, I looked at the ceiling, the bed steadily moving down the hallway, James on one side and the nurse on the other. When we reached the doorway to the waiting area, James' parents were standing in view, blowing me kisses and holding up their thumbs, index fingers, and pinky fingers, sign language for "I love you."

Before being moved into the operating room (OR), Dr. Zempolich came to talk to us. I started to feel more nervous. Not because the procedure scared me, but what might come of it. "Glad to see we all got here safe," she said, sounding relieved for herself. "I have some forms I need you to sign, but first, I need to ask you a few questions." She handed me a clipboard with several consents. What she asked next was something I'd not prepared myself for. "Now, if I find any obvious signs of cancer, do you consent to me removing anything I see?"

I immediately looked at James, thinking he could answer for me. I'd not given any thought to the idea this day could result in anything more than a biopsy, let alone the removal of any part of me meant for creating or carrying life. *How could she even know for certain what was going on without running pathology?* How was I supposed to be expected to make this decision, only moments before entering the OR?

"What do you think?" I asked James. Resentful my situation already felt completely out of my control, I needed his help to know what to do.

"That isn't a decision I can make for you, babe," James said, stroking my hand. Dr. Zempolich nodded. I knew this was going to be up to me.

"I guess if you're absolutely certain something is wrong, you can do whatever you feel is best, but if you can give me more time to decide,

I'd much rather decide later." I heard the doubt in my voice as I said the words.

She wrote down my answer and placed another paper on the clipboard in my lap. Knowing what signing meant, this one extra page felt heavier with a weight I hadn't anticipated carrying. I signed my name as neatly as I could.

I kissed James goodbye, and he squeezed my hand three times, our quiet way of saying "I love you." I gave four deep squeezes back, "I love you, too." Waiting outside the operating room, a few doctors and nurses walked by. Some smiled at me, some looked away, and a few offered me a warm blanket. Of course, I didn't refuse.

After a short wait, the anesthesiologist pushed me into the OR. Being on my back, I didn't have much chance to see my surroundings. I was only able to see the bright fluorescent light directly above the table. Feeling the cold air circulating around me, I was immediately thankful for my warm blankets. In normal fashion, I tried my hardest to fight the sensation of sleep that came over me once the medications were injected. But, as usual, I lost the battle and as I slipped away, I said, "Good luck, have fun, bye."

Another dreamless sleep slowly came to an end. It felt like I'd simultaneously been asleep for hours but also barely closed my eyes. Regaining consciousness, I had no idea how long I'd been out, couldn't feel my body, and didn't know where I was. My heavy eyelids slowly lifted and closed in a much more consistent cadence as each moment passed.

As if underwater, I could hear the muffled sound of people above me talking. I looked to my left and saw the outline of a nurse hooking and unhooking wires to the machines next to my bed. Slowly turning my head to the right, I felt a sudden jolt bring me fully to consciousness. Dr. Zempolich stood at the foot of my bed, softly speaking to the nurse. I'd woken from anesthesia enough times to know it couldn't be a good sign to see her standing there. Before she even knew I was awake, I blurted out in a panic, "Did you find something?"

Startled by my sudden alertness and question, her conversation with the nurse ended abruptly. She took in a breath, squeezing my foot tenderly. Her hand gently ran up my leg and she approached the head of the bed. Her facial expression showed deep compassion.

"Yes, dear," she said, her hand now resting on top of mine. "It's stage three ovarian cancer. And there's a lot."

I felt like a bucket of ice-cold water had been dumped over my head as I tried to catch my breath. Before the words even exited her lips, my eyes filled with tears. "No, I don't want to die!" I shouted.

I broke our gaze to look for James. He wasn't there. I started to panic and cried even harder, beginning to hyperventilate.

She guided my attention back to her, holding my face between her slightly cold hands, trying to calm me. "You're not going to die," she said, staring me right in the eye. "We are going to beat this."

"James? Does he know? Where is he?" I asked frantically, ignoring her reassuring words. My crying became uncontrollable. I looked around to see other patients lying in their beds, also waking from anesthesia. Some were alert enough to have witnessed this news being broken to me. Dr. Zempolich instructed the nurse to take me to my room where James waited.

I was immediately wheeled toward the door, passing other patients who looked at me with pity. I started to feel angry at and disgusted by my body. How could I be thirty-four years old and have cancer? I wanted to rip it out immediately and not let it have one more moment to thrive on my organs. By the time I got to my room, I was certain the entire hospital had heard my sobs.

The instant my bed entered the room James sprang out of his chair and held my hand. I could see the redness and swelling in his eyes. He kissed my forehead, and we hugged while letting fear, sadness, and anger wash over us. We'd never held each other so tightly nor felt such exhaustion and grief.

A few moments later, James' parents came into the room. His mom approached me first. She wrapped her hands around my face, "I am so sorry, my sweet Jenny girl. I love you so much," she said, kissing my forehead.

James' dad made his way to my side. Tears freely fell from his eyes, leaving small water spots on his shirt. His face was pain-stricken, and he could barely speak. He hugged me in such a way I never would have guessed I wasn't one of his own children. "I am so sorry, Jenny," he managed to whisper in my ear. I could feel his body tremble while he put his head on my shoulder.

After James's parents left, I called my mom. She'd told me several times over the years how guilty she would feel if any of her kids with the BRCA mutation were diagnosed with cancer. I knew this was going to be a difficult call. I was exhausted and hadn't emotionally caught up to what was happening. She answered the phone on the first ring, "What did they find?" I could hear the worry in her tone.

"Mom, they found cancer." Having not yet talked with James, I was unable to answer her immediate questions about what the doctor had said, what my treatment would be, or what their outlook was. She started to cry, and I could feel her sadness through the phone. The call ended rather quickly as I could tell she didn't want to become emotional in front of me.

James recounted what he'd experienced while waiting for me with his parents. "About thirty minutes in, Dr. Zempolich came into the waiting room and called me over to a small, private room off to the side," he said, speaking softly yet slowly. "I knew it couldn't be good."

"James," she began, just the two of them sitting together, "I found cancer. And there was a lot. It started in her ovaries and has spread throughout her abdomen." She tenderly reached for his hand. She presented him with several images she'd printed.

"These are her ovaries," she pointed to two enlarged spheres, covered with a white, icing-like substance. "They shouldn't be touching, but the cancer, this white stuff here, is binding them together. It is hard to tell if they are stuck to her uterus, which is right here." She flipped the page over. "This is her liver and diaphragm. These little specks are also cancer. Imagine the cancer was a dandelion and someone blew on it. These little spots are like the seeds that blow away." Setting the pictures down, she asked James the question we'd not been prepared to answer.

"Do you want me to go in and remove all of the cancer I can see?"

To James, it felt as though the world stood still for a moment. He felt a heaviness on his shoulders at the prospect of making such a monumental decision for not only me, but for his future as well. "Is there any danger in allowing her to wake up and letting us decide this together?" he asked.

"I don't think there's any large risk of the cancer spreading more if we wake her today." she assured him. "However, I wouldn't wait more than a week or two to get back in so we can get it out. I think that's our best bet at beating this."

A few hours after waking, I was discharged from the hospital and sent out into the world as though my life hadn't just been flipped upside down. We still had to scrape the snow off the car in the parking lot, had to stop at all the traffic lights, and were forced to move at a snail's pace through the heavy flow of rush hour. Nothing changed because I'd suddenly learned I had cancer. I couldn't fathom how our day started so hopeful with the news of our little EmbryLowe and ended in the cruelest way possible.

While driving home, still in shock, I called my siblings to tell them. This wasn't something I felt I could sit on for several hours, and knowing my mom, they would know before long. I spoke to my older brother who lives in California first.

"I have cancer," I blurted out when he answered. I didn't have the energy to sugarcoat the delivery because no one had done so for me. Even if they had, it isn't a word I imagine is often received softly. I could hear the fear in his voice as I finished telling him what little I knew.

I spoke to my sister next. Despite our eleven-year age difference and that she also lived in California, we were extremely close. Sniffling on the other end of the phone, I felt her fear and heartbreak. Also being positive for the BRCA 1 mutation, she'd recently had a preventative double mastectomy. Ovarian cancer scared her, but much like me she hadn't been as concerned about it. This reality made her not only sad for me but also scared for the risks she faced as well.

Lastly, I FaceTimed my oldest brother, who lived only fifteen minutes away from us. Looking back at me from the screen, I saw the same look of sadness and grief that was becoming familiar to me.

"Can I come over?" my brother asked, almost immediately after I finished speaking. I hadn't been able to tell them much before the call ended, and he was on his way to my house. When he arrived, James answered the door. No words were spoken, and from upstairs, I heard them embrace along with a lot of manly pats on the back.

"Thank you for coming over," I heard James say. My brother came up the stairs, and his gaze met mine. He walked over, hugged me intensely, as only an older brother can, and I sobbed into his shirt.

"It will be okay. You are going to be okay," he said, rubbing the back of my head.

James' parents brought us dinner, despite my not being in any mood to eat. The thought of providing fuel for this growing disease made me ill. Additionally, they insisted on shoveling our driveway, as it hadn't stopped snowing all day.

"You know, we pay a homeowner's association fee so someone else will come and do that," James said, trying to stop them from exerting their energy.

"I know. Please let us do this," his mom said, zipping her jacket and reaching for a shovel. "There isn't much else we can do, and sometimes you just want to help."

Sitting in the house, in one of the few quiet and contemplative moments I'd yet to have all day, I was hypnotized by the sound of shovels scraping across the driveway. For a moment, my mind was clear and not thinking about cancer, but focused on how the snow was being removed from where it didn't belong. I was immediately sad when they stopped, as it propelled me back into the reality of what the day had brought. I only hoped my surfaces could similarly be wiped clean.

The rest of the evening was filled with more phone calls and tears. Nothing prepares you to tell someone you love that you have cancer. One would think after speaking the words "I have cancer" as many times as I did that day, it would sink in and start to seem real. However, the exact opposite happened. I found myself repeating the word cancer so many times it became one of those words that sounds strange the more you say it, like fork.

I realized this was the beginning of a new chapter in my life, defined by one word. I felt myself becoming numb to the reality that this was happening and my journey to becoming a mother was now the last thing I could focus on. Maybe that was a good thing. Perhaps the more desensitized I was in the beginning, the easier it would be to overcome. I only wish it would have been that simple.

CHAPTER 8

The next few days blurred together. Between the calls and texts, I felt exhausted sharing my diagnosis and eventually put my phone away to avoid becoming more overwhelmed. I didn't know how I was going to manage the additional physical toll of surgery and chemo as well as getting things settled with insurance and work.

Friday morning, two days after my biopsy, James and I pulled into the office parking lot of a marriage counselor we'd been seeing for several months. We'd both spent several years receiving individual therapy, and I was thankful James shared my strong belief in the value of working to better oneself.

It seemed only natural to seek ways we could work on our relationship and communication as a couple. The time we'd spent talking with someone had thus far proven to be instrumental in our marriage's success, and we agreed the news of my cancer would undoubtedly present trials we couldn't face alone.

I pulled the car into one of the few open stalls, put it in park, and let out an exhausted sigh. I knew the upcoming conversation was going to be emotionally draining, and I didn't know if I felt strong enough to get through it.

Just as I pulled the keys out of the ignition, my phone rang, and Dr. Zempolich's name came on the screen. We both knew this was an important call that would help determine the next steps for treatment.

"Jen, no matter what happens," James said, taking my hand and looking directly into my eyes, "you are going to fight this, and you are going to win."

James was an eternal optimist, almost to a fault. He always tried to see the positive in every situation, and I'd always been much the opposite. I not only saw things in a negative light often, but I was also anxious and worried about things I had no control over. My negativity was not my way of choosing sadness, but rather, attempting to protect myself from being hurt when my expectations were not met. Years of therapy have taught me pessimism is difficult to overcome. I smiled at him, not completely sure I shared the same sentiment, and pushed the green button to answer.

During the first few moments she described the results of my pathology report. I had stage three ovarian cancer throughout my abdomen and colon. She explained the stages are based on whether the cancer had spread to other parts of the body, which in my case, it had.

"Really, you have two options," she said. "The first would be to complete three rounds of chemo to shrink any existing cancer, followed by surgery to remove any cancer we can still see, and finish with three more rounds of chemo."

This option gave me hope that by shrinking the cancer first, I might be able to keep my uterus and could possibly still get pregnant someday. "Your ovaries were very swollen and appeared to be adhered to your uterus, leaving me uncertain about what we can salvage. However, this is a common and effective treatment plan." I trusted the optimism and confidence I heard in her voice as she assured me of this plan's efficacy.

"The second option would be to get you into surgery as soon as possible, remove everything we see, and then complete all six rounds of chemo after that. Although I am confident in my ability to remove all the cancer, I can't promise you, in either scenario, I will be able to save your uterus," she said, indicating my decision might not make a difference either way. "Having surgery first would merely help our understanding of where the cancer had spread."

To say I didn't know how to proceed is an understatement. Part of me was so hopeful I would still be healthy enough to experience pregnancy and carry our sweet EmbryLowe one day. Part of me feared she was being overly optimistic and ultimately this decision would be out of my hands. "What would you suggest I do?" I asked, wishing the answer could be simple, but knowing again she wouldn't be able to make it for me.

"I can't say for sure, but if we are able to keep the uterus and you want to attempt to get pregnant someday, I have to caution it could be years until that is possible." My head fell back onto the headrest, and I could hear my heart pounding in my temples.

"After you complete chemo, you'll likely be on a daily medication for at least five years, and it wouldn't be safe for you to take it while pregnant. Having a baby right away would not be advisable."

I looked at James, who stared out the window, nodding his head slowly and blinking. I closed my eyes and envisioned myself walking through a tunnel. Instead of walking toward the small speck of light I saw at the end, I was being pulled toward the darkness. It felt as though someone had taken my hand and was forcing me to go in the opposite direction. I wanted to scream out for help but knew it was no use because there was no way anyone would hear me or any way to turn around.

"I know this isn't what you want to hear after all you have been going through, and I will support either decision you make," Dr. Zempolich said. "But my recommendation would be to have a full hysterectomy and then complete the chemo." This cut me deeply.

The finality of the word *hysterectomy* made my chest tighten, and I momentarily felt like the wind had been knocked out of me. I was only thirty-four years old and being told my best option for survival was to remove the only chance I had to carry a child. I never imagined having to make this decision, let alone at the time I finally felt ready to become a mother. I'd never felt devastation like this before.

I didn't feel I needed to discuss it further with James, knowing he likely felt the same way and would support me no matter what decision I made. Sitting in my Subaru Forester, outside our marriage therapist's office, I made one of the most difficult decisions of my life.

"Based on what you've told me, I think moving forward with surgery, then chemo is probably the right thing to do." I glanced at James to see his reaction. Tears fell from his eyes. "The thought of allowing this cancer to stay in my body any longer has kept me awake over the last few nights." As much as I wanted to have a baby, I could more easily forgive myself for giving up that possibility if it meant I would have a better chance to be alive. I wasn't sure when I would forgive myself, but I knew I would eventually.

"This seems like a really silly question, given the heaviness of everything else we are discussing, but will this chemo cause me to lose all my hair?" I was confident I already knew the answer. The thought of losing my hair also kept me awake. It felt like one more cruel twist to this already unfair and uncontrollable situation.

"Unfortunately. Yes, you will," she said. I found it hard to look James in the eyes, but finally met his gaze. He exhaled, reaching over to wipe the tears now running down my cheek. Silence lingered, and my shaky voice finally interrupted. "How soon will that happen?" I asked, trying my hardest to stay composed and graceful.

"Once you start chemo, it will be about two weeks until it falls out," she answered, with a direct, yet sympathetic tone. I hung my head in defeat. This time, she interrupted the silence. "We are going to get all this cancer out, and you're going to beat this." I felt a calm wash over me knowing I was able to get on her schedule for surgery twelve days later.

Hanging up, I hadn't ever been more thankful for a therapy appointment in my life.

CHAPTER 9

I've found when faced with heartbreak and pain, it's often difficult to not become overwhelmed by the full picture of the road that lies ahead. It can feel damn near impossible to view challenges one day, or a moment, at a time. Over the next week, I couldn't stop thinking about what I was now losing in terms of becoming a mother. I also became extremely intimidated about a major surgery followed by undergoing chemo. It felt like I would fight this battle for an eternity, and I hadn't even started yet.

With each new day, I reminded myself, out loud, that although I was mourning and scared I needed to do my best to only focus on what I could control in each moment. Sometimes it was hour to hour, and others, minute to minute. Although difficult to always remember, it became an important practice for me to maintain positivity.

The Saturday before my surgery I went to the gym for what I knew would be the last time in a while. Going to the gym had become a normal part of my weekly routine over the last three years. I worked out four days a week and was stronger than I'd ever been. I was afraid to lose all the progress I'd worked so hard for. I worried the familiarity and capability I'd gained would be taken away along with my ovaries and the cancer.

Holding a pair of forty-pound weights between a set of chest presses, I looked in the mirror at the woman staring back and started to sob. I didn't care if anyone saw the emotion erupting from my body. This would be the last time I'd be capable of completing a task as seemingly easy as lying on my back and pushing the weight upwards—and the last time I'd get annoyed at my hair for falling out of the loose ponytail it was tied in or my bicep would look as sculpted as it did. Music from my workout playlist blared from my earbuds, and nameless, yet familiar faces of other gym goers, continued working out around me. They had no way of knowing what was about to happen to me or how this might be the last time they saw me. I set the weights down and cried into my hands. *This isn't fucking fair.*

That night, to lift my spirits, James asked to take me on a date. After my experience at the gym, I was reluctant, feeling exhausted and fragile.

"I want to take you on a 'James and Jenny' tour," he said, explaining his desire to visit a few places special to us.

Around six o'clock we were on our way to the first location. Not far from our house, James pulled into a small parking lot of a breakfast cafe where he'd eaten with his dad on the morning of our wedding. He explained how meaningful the experience had been to have one-on-one time before vowing to be my husband.

"I don't know if I am going to be able to handle more sentiment tonight!" I said as we left the parking lot and headed to our next secret location. We drove a familiar path that made me believe we were going to his parent's house, but at the last minute, took a turn in another direction. I realized where we might be going.

James pulled into the parking lot of a non-denominational community church where we'd held our rehearsal dinner the night before our wedding. He slowed the car and approached the building, distracting me with reasons this venue held special meaning to him. *There must be an event going on tonight.* I wiped my eyes and noticed several cars in the parking lot. I lost focus on what James was saying as teal-colored balloons caught my attention through the undraped windows.

"I wonder what is going on," I said. I thought it a strange coincidence the balloons were teal, having recently learned this was the color of the ovarian cancer ribbon.

"Wait, is that my parents' car... and your parents' car?" More than a few of the vehicles were familiar. I hadn't noticed James already on his way to open my door after putting the car in park along the curb. For the second time that day, I cradled my face in my palms and cried.

James led me to the door, allowing me to pause a few times and gather my emotions. Not being totally certain who waited for me inside, I assumed it would be only a few close friends and family. I walked through the door and nearly dropped to my knees. My vision was blurred, making it impossible to see all the faces in front of me.

"Surprise!" the group yelled in unison. Roughly seventy-five people from different places and times in my life stared back at me. They were all dressed in a shade of teal and had ribbons pinned to their shirts.

"Speech! Speech!" my brother-in-law yelled, attempting to alleviate my shock.

I was speechless and almost embarrassed at all the attention. How did I even know this many people? How had James pulled this off without me knowing? I always prided myself in being somewhat of a sleuth and couldn't believe he'd organized this without me having any bit of suspicion. In fact, my ability to ruin a surprise had caused a few arguments over the years. I couldn't stand to not know details of something I sensed was coming, so I had often pressed for answers. Now I turned and leaned into James, like a shy child not wanting to let go of their parent.

"I can't believe you did this!" I whispered, the clicking of a camera and sounds of others crying swirled around me. It was one of the most touching moments of my life.

They'd all gathered in one place to show their love and support as I prepared to embark on the most difficult journey of my life. The room was decorated with not only balloons, but years of memories I'd made with each person in attendance. Family, high school friends, fellow corgi lovers, coworkers, and friends we played with on our adult recreation league kickball team.

I walked around the room and hugged every individual, laughing with some and crying with others.

Having been to several funerals in my life, I often morbidly wondered what kind of attendance there would be at mine someday. I felt as though my ridiculous question was answered that night. I'd always known I had friends and family who cared for and loved me, but seeing them all together in one room was a support I'd never felt, nor one I realized I would need.

CHAPTER 10

The following Wednesday, February 20, after a rather restless sleep, James and I made the early bleary-eyed drive to the hospital. This time, there was no snow, but instead, a cloudless night was coming to an end as the stars and moon offered a soft blue light in the sky. James placed my overnight bag, filled with odds and ends to help keep me occupied, in the trunk while I buckled myself in.

When I come home, part of me will be missing, and I will never be whole again. As the car backed out of the driveway, I couldn't bring myself to acknowledge this thought out loud, already trying to keep my fears at bay.

A familiar scene played out when I entered the hospital lobby to check in. James' parents were again sitting in the waiting room. I felt a large sense of deja vu being led back into my pre-op room, having just been through this routine only two weeks earlier. I was quickly offered the coveted warm blankets, and thirty minutes after I settled in, my parents walked into my room.

Approaching my bed, my mom asked, "Hi honey. How are you feeling?" She knew all too well what I was going through, having been here herself. She didn't have much to say but stood quietly at my side to stroke away the stray hairs on my forehead. I was happy she was there to support me. After all, there is nothing in the world quite like a mother's support.

The time came to go upstairs, and I was wheeled down the same hallway as before. This time, my parents stood alongside my in-laws in the doorway, waving and blowing kisses. James held my hand the entire way.

I was wheeled into a small room next to the OR to await one final conversation with Dr. Zempolich before the surgery got under way. She entered shortly afterward. Her dark hair was pulled back into a ponytail, accentuating strands of gray wisped throughout. Her calming smile immediately reduced my building anxiety. She handed me several familiar consent forms and a few new ones.

Before the ink was dry, she left the room to give James and me a moment alone to say goodbye. I tried to not put much weight into thinking something could go wrong, but the fear crept in.

"I am so scared," I said. He kissed me and squeezed my hand three times. I knew he was scared too.

Before the surgery began, I needed to have an epidural placed, which could only be administered while I was awake. I'd always assumed I would only need an epidural during labor when I wouldn't care how badly it might hurt to have the small catheter slipped into my spine. I felt my pulse beginning to speed up at the thought.

The nurse wheeled me into the OR, and I was immediately struck by the cool air flowing through the vents. I sat upright and was instructed to dangle my legs over the side of the table I had just moved to. The nurse introduced herself and a few of the other technicians, names I would unfortunately forget moments later. I realized this was the first glimpse I'd ever had of an operating room. I felt like a newborn seeing shapes and colors for the first time, not able to focus on one thing for long before shifting attention to something else.

Several large machines buzzed and beeped loudly. I had no idea what any of them were and was thankful someone else did. Sterile operating instruments lined a metal tray next to the table. The lights were bright but did little to offer any kind of warmth. There were several doors leading in and out of the room. I envisioned secret tunnels and passageways surgeons might use to navigate their way through the hospital.

"Okay, Jennifer, let's get this epidural in," the anesthesiologist said, rather enthusiastically. "I am going to need you to hunch your shoulders and crouch over this pillow. Also, hold still. You will feel some popping and pressure when I insert the catheter."

I let out a deep breath and tried to shake myself of the fear that pulsed through my body. A young female nurse stood in front of me to help keep me still. "Can I please hold your hand?" I asked, reaching to her, for support. She led my breath through the pain and used her free hand to softly wipe my tears before they fell onto my gown.

Once the epidural was placed, two nurses slowly lifted my legs from the side of the table and helped me lower myself onto my back. A few more people entered the room, and I could sense the energy shifting from preparation to action. They were ready to start, and all that was missing was Dr. Zempolich. I looked at the digital clock located above one of the doors. It was 12:00 p.m., on the dot. I took a few deep breaths, knowing the medications were now working their way through my veins. Again, I tried to fight them, but my eyes got heavy, my vision began to blur. "Have fun," I said as I drifted off.

The next thing I knew, I was being moved down a long hallway. Feeling paralyzed, the only movement I could manage was opening and closing my eyes. I felt dizzy, lying on my back, looking at ceiling panels and light fixtures as they passed and faded images of two nurses pulling my bed. I heard my name a few times, but couldn't give a response with my throat still scratchy from the tube that had just been removed. I heard one of the nurses say "ICU" and the other nurse used the word "soiled."

One of my biggest, yet irrational fears about giving birth someday, was pooping on the table while I pushed. Knowing this is a common thing to happen never made me feel much better about the prospect. I was not afraid to leave the door open at home, yet for some reason I felt self-conscious and worried about what else would come out while the doctor was face-to-face with my undercarriage while delivering a baby.

It didn't take me long to realize my fear had come to fruition. I didn't have any control of my bowels and had just shit on myself without any warning or indication it was happening.

"I shit?" I asked, although so softly, I don't think the nurses heard. My stomach turned with guilt over the scene as this had to be the most disgusting thing a nurse could ever witness. However, I realized it wasn't guilt I felt, but my bowels releasing more excrement. We made it to my room in the intensive care unit (ICU), a place I had never been or expected to be.

Still groggy, I made eye contact with James, standing within view. I felt the nervousness leave my body the moment I saw him, but realized yet again, it was my out-of-control bowels. I felt ashamed and embarrassed about what he was witnessing, but he didn't give it a second thought. He immediately kissed my swollen forehead, later telling me I'd been unrecognizably bloated from the nine liters of fluid I required during surgery.

"Sorry, James. I crapped on myself. I think it is happening again right now," I said in a strung-out, slurred attempt at a sentence.

I looked around the room and saw a round, black and white clock hanging on the wall. I blinked several times, trying to focus my eyes. *That can't be right.*

"Seven-thirty?" I asked, certain I was still sedated enough to have read it incorrectly.

"That's right," a slender red-haired nurse said. She'd been tasked with cleaning my mess, and I could feel her wiping my butt. *Poor girl.*

"My surgery lasted seven and a half hours?" Shocked at this realization. I couldn't believe I'd been in surgery that long. Between the hysterectomy and abdominal exploration, Dr. Zempolich indicated she thought it would only take three to four hours. When I was finally a little more awake, James was able to tell me why it took so long.

"They found a lot more cancer than they expected," he said, holding my hand. "They removed your ovaries, cervix, uterus, appendix, two lymph nodes, part of your liver, part of your diaphragm, and about three inches of your bowels." There was no way I would remember all of it. "She also took your small intestines out and went through them inch by inch to ensure there was no cancer in them." *No wonder my bowels were going crazy!*

Over the next hour, I had four more bouts of unwanted diarrhea. It felt like as soon as the nurse cleaned me, I was calling her back in again only moments later. I eventually refused to push the call button until I knew I wasn't going to go again so quickly. I was certain she had more important things to attend to in the ICU than my muddy ass.

This room was different from other hospital rooms I'd been in. There was no traditional door at the entrance, but a sliding glass door the length of the wall. A curtain, not quite long enough to touch the ground, stretched the entire width of the glass wall, letting light seep through. A toilet sat in the corner, draped by a similar curtain to offer privacy.

Every time I moved I became entangled in the mess of wires attached to my monitors. I had two IVs placed in each arm, a urinary catheter with a not-so-subtle collection bag, a chest tube preventing fluid from going into my lungs, a heart-rate monitor attached to my finger, and socks hooked to a device intermittently compressing my legs to prevent blood clots. I felt bionic, half-human, half-machine.

The following morning, around five o'clock, I awakened abruptly from the sound of several technicians entering my room. The curtain was pulled back, with urgency, and lights were flipped on. I had no time to acclimate to the change in brightness before being propped up by an x-ray tech trying to put a board behind my back.

"Is there any chance you could be pregnant?" he asked, while jostling me into the right position.

James jumped out of the lounger bed, his blanket falling to the floor. He had not realized he was only wearing his underwear as he rushed to my side. I'd been startled, and my heart rate monitor beeped furiously, like Morse code.

"Really?" James said, snapping at the tech. "Did you not look at her chart at all? She just had a hysterectomy." The tech halfheartedly apologized for the mistake and proceeded with the task at hand. Unfortunately, this was not the last morning I would be awoken to get an x-ray, nor was it the last time someone would ask if I could be pregnant.

The unrest in the ICU continued. Between visits from a few family members and various doctors constantly checking on me, I was not able to get much-needed sleep to recover. I was unbelievably hungry and even more thirsty but wasn't allowed to have anything to eat or drink, other than ice chips, which James fed me with a spoon.

When our parents visited, I was too tired to even speak to them. Instead, sitting in silence, all four of them constantly looked at my heart rate and oxygen monitor every time it beeped. Unable to relax, I became obsessed with watching my vitals rise and fall.

On Friday, my second full day in the ICU, a rehab nurse came into my room. He was tall and muscular, with dark curly hair pulled into a messy bun. "We're going to get you to try to stand and walk today," he said optimistically.

Although exhausted, I agreed to try. He pressed the button on the bed to slowly bring me to a sitting position. I hadn't fully sat up since surgery. The blood rushed from my head, my heart beat through my skull, and black spots momentarily interrupted my vision. After a few moments upright, I began to feel normal and draped my legs over the side of the bed.

"On the count of three, I'm going to help you stand, and when you're ready, we're going to walk four or five steps to that chair over there." He pointed at the so-called bed James had slept on for the last two nights. "One... two... three." He steadied my arms and bore most of my weight while I slowly put my feet on the floor. I used what little leg and core strength I could manage to stand, something I'd done every day and now strained to do.

I immediately felt lightheaded and began to sway. "I'm going to pass out!" I said, my body tingling. He gently helped me back into a seated position and guided my breathing to help ensure I wouldn't faint. Thoughts swirled through my mind, much like the various swirls of light I now saw in front of me. *Oh my God, I'm never going to be able to stand again.*

"You did well," he said. I scoffed. I'd hardly stood for two seconds before needing to bail. "Let's try again tomorrow."

My incision, which measured roughly twelve inches long and went from the bottom of my rib cage to the top of my pelvis, was restricting and painful. I wore a tightly cinched chest wrap to ensure my skin could heal and my swelling would go down. It was difficult to breathe or move, and on top of that, I felt disgusting having not showered or brushed my hair in three days.

The next evening, my nurse came in to check on me. She'd worked the night before but hadn't been assigned to me. I'd met her when she came into my room to answer a question while my nurse was busy with another patient. Our first encounter was pleasant, and she was extremely attentive and kind. She would prove to be my favorite caregiver.

While becoming acquainted, I started to cry describing how dirty and gross I felt. "Well, you are in luck!" she said, her smile beaming light in a moment of my darkness. "You see, I'm an expert hair washer and braider. I would love nothing more than to get you all clean and feeling fresh." She left the room for a moment, only to return with her hands full of essential body cleaning supplies. "I've got baby wipes, a toothbrush and toothpaste, dry shampoo, a brush, and some deodorant here for you. How does that sound?" I couldn't prop myself fast enough in excitement at the display of goodies she set on the table.

She dimmed the lights, and for the next thirty minutes, cleaned my skin, brushed my teeth, and massaged my shoulders. Additionally, she took time to wash, brush, and braid my hair, while offering conversation and laughter I was in desperate need of to feel human. I couldn't believe how such a small act helped me forget for a moment I had cancer and was sitting in an ICU.

On Sunday morning, my rehab nurse, hair still tied back in the same messy bun, came back one more time before I was moved to a new room. I was initially overcome with dread watching him prepare my bedside for another attempt at standing. I'd felt so incapable and weak the day before, I wasn't sure I was physically or emotionally up for the task again.

He counted to three, again bracing me as I tried to rise to my feet. This time, I felt my weight shift to my legs, which held me steady. Standing in one place for sixty seconds, I didn't have the urge to pass out and began to slowly move toward the chair. Completely out of breath, I made it just in time to sit and take a rest. I knew it wasn't a giant leap for mankind, but it was a significant step for me.

CHAPTER 11

I t felt like Christmas morning when I was finally moved out of the ICU on Sunday afternoon. This would mean I would be able to introduce solid foods back into my life, having only been allowed Sprite and apple juice up to this point. Not only that, but there was an actual door to both the entrance and the bathroom in my new room, my home for the next several days of recovery. I was moving on up!

My excitement over my new digs was met with many ups and downs. I was still in a lot of pain, and medications didn't seem to be working as well. In fact, upon arriving at my new address, I'd expected the nurses would check on me as often as they had in the ICU. At one moment, I felt my medications beginning to wear off and I pushed the call button to ask for my next dose.

The nurse, a gray-haired, heavy-set woman in her mid-forties, shuffled into the room, a scowl on her face. I asked kindly how often she was supposed to be giving me my medications. "This isn't the ICU, honey. You have to ask for them, I can't read your mind." *Wow, why are you such a bitch?*

I learned quickly that a nurse or doctor could make or break an entire patient experience. Having never required someone to attend to my every need, I was not used to frequently asking for help. In moments when James had to be elsewhere, I became surprised at how hesitant I was to ask a nurse for assistance, out of fear they didn't have the time or patience.

Sunday evening, I felt a great deal of pain where an IV had been nestled in my vein for nearly five days. It began to burn at the injection site as the medication entered my body. I rang the button for the nurse. Ten minutes later, the same ornery woman entered my room, her breathing labored from the walk.

"What is it?" she said with a huff, clearly annoyed I'd called for help.

"This IV is really bothering me," I said, holding my left arm to show her the redness and swelling. "I wonder if you can change it for me."

She bent down to get a closer look. I could feel the heat of her breath on my arm as she poked at the dressing. "It looks fine to me," she said, dismissively. "We don't need to change it."

"Are you sure? It really hurts." I grasped my arm attempting to alleviate the pain.

"No, changing it wouldn't help. Just try not to move your arm so much." I sat in shock watching her silhouette disappear. I couldn't believe how she'd written me off and left me to suffer. I didn't push my button for the rest of the evening, not even for pain medications, out of fear I couldn't handle another interaction with her.

The following day, after the shift change, I casually mentioned to my new nurse the pain in my arm. She carefully examined the site and agreed it looked as though it had possibly been in one spot for too long. Before I knew it, she had a new IV kit in her hand and prepared to remove and replace it.

"I asked the nurse last night if she could move it and she said no!" I told her, still in disbelief over my encounter.

"Between you and me," she whispered, leaning in to avoid anyone overhearing her, "she isn't big on putting in IVs and will refuse to do them as much as possible." It made me wonder why someone would choose nursing as their profession if they didn't seem to like their job.

I often slept with eight or nine pillows on my bed to help prop certain parts of my body and relieve pressure. Ice packs covered me from head to toe as I experienced my first signs of early menopause and hot flashes, caused by my hysterectomy. My daily emotional breakdowns continued, often in front of nurses. Small tasks still seemed daunting.

I just wanted to go home and be in my own bed, cuddled with James and Gus. The food was harder to eat than I thought it would be, based on my level of hunger. And even though I felt hungry, I didn't often feel like eating the slightly warm lasagna or cold Jell-O they brought me.

Monday evening, while sitting with a few girlfriends, I started to feel pain and asked the nurse for my medications. After waiting thirty minutes for her to arrive, she administered all of them at once, causing me to suddenly feel a rush of nausea. It wasn't the first time my friends held my hair while I puked, nor probably the last.

After my visitors left, a new nurse I'd not seen before entered the room. "Hi Jennifer, I'm Grace, your nurse for the evening," she said. She looked to be in her late twenties and had big brown eyes not easy to miss.

"Before I start treating you, I want to first make sure you are comfortable with me being your nurse tonight," she said.

"Do I know you?" I asked, racking my brain for familiarity. Maybe I knew her from high school or church? Maybe she thinks it would be awkward if she was in here and I am basically naked under this gown?

I'd once gone in for a mammogram only to find the tech was a girl I'd grown up with but hadn't seen in several years. Before starting the exam, she asked if I was okay with her doing the test, since she would see and feel my boobs. Although thoughtful of her to ensure I was comfortable, I indicated it was fine. After all, she had boobs, too. They can't be that different.

Thinking maybe this was a similar situation, I continued to search my mind for how I might know her. "Jen, she is pregnant," James said, pointing at her budding belly. I'd not even noticed this major detail when she entered the room. The dim lighting and her scrubs made it difficult to see.

"I just want to make sure you're okay, because I know you just had a hysterectomy, and I don't want my presence to upset you." This was yet another example of someone who was kind, empathetic, and considerate, a stark contrast to the ignorance and insensitivity displayed by the x-ray techs only days before. Obviously, she also became one of my favorites.

The following day, now six days post-surgery, brought a new development. I was told I could go home as soon as I had a bowel movement. I was successfully getting out of bed on my own, without feeling like I was going to pass out, and with the help of a walker, I'd been taking walks around the floor several times a day. I started out slow, from one end of the hall to the other. Then I was able to complete an entire lap around the nurse's station, followed by multiple laps before getting tired and needing to rest. This was supposed to help my bowels recover and regulate back to normal.

I hadn't had a bowel movement since my dam broke in the ICU. Between walking and eating solid food, the goal and requirement for me to leave the hospital was now to poop voluntarily. I'd never wanted to poop so badly, and it became my new focus.

That evening, James was getting ready to head home for the night, the makeshift couch-bed being two feet shorter than him and uncomfortable to sleep on. I struggled to get out of the pit of pillows that swallowed me like quicksand but finally got comfortable on my right side. With my left leg hiked up, as if in the fetal position, a loud fart suddenly escaped my butt.

"Did you just fart?" James asked. It was the first time I'd heard excitement in his tone accompanying that question.

"Yes!" I screamed, pushing one more time to see if there was another one in the chamber.

"Good job, babe! I'm so excited for you!" James said, kissing my forehead and rubbing my leg. In that exact moment, I felt movement in my bowels, the kind I'd not felt in days, but knew was more than a fart.

"Oh no, call the nurse! I think I'm about to blow!" I cried out, reaching frantically for the call button. I urgently informed the nurse on the other end I was going to need assistance. I knew I wasn't going to make it to the bathroom in time. This was NOT a drill. The pressure and the pain in my stomach became suddenly and unbearably intense.

"Babe, I need you to hold my leg." I moved James' hand to my upper thigh to hold it in place as a cramp left me breathless. "I feel like it's stuck. Can you help spread my butt cheeks and see if anything happens?" I asked in desperation. I didn't know what else might relieve me of this pain, but I wanted to try anything I could. He put his hand on my now bare left cheek and pulled it to the side. Immediately, my bowels emptied all over my bed.

"Great job, you are doing so well," James said, looking me right in the eye. He cheered me on as if I was in labor pushing out a baby. I could feel the warmth of the shit under my body, and it felt like it wasn't stopping.

"I am so sorry, James," I kept repeating, even though happy to be having my first bowel movement. I'd never in my life felt more vulnerable than I did in that moment. I never expected my husband would need to hold my butt to help me poop, at least not until I was in my nineties.

Unprepared to be so involved, James had not been wearing gloves, nor had time to put any sort of pad down to help collect the mess that followed. Once I felt safe to say I was done, he walked out of the room to see if he could find the nurse I'd called. Unable to find anyone, he came back into the room and started going through the cupboards to find supplies to help clean me.

"James, please. You already had to endure that. You're *not* cleaning me up, too." I was horrified.

"You literally have black tar all over you. I'm not going to let you sit in that mess." He opened and closed every cabinet in the room. A few moments later, equipped with all he needed, he began to wipe my ass, change my sheets, and dress me in a new robe. It was an intimacy I hadn't ever experienced. It wasn't sexy nor did it involve the kind of physical contact one would expect. However, it was one of the most compassionate and deeply moving moments of my life to have the man I married, living his vow to love and care for me through sickness and health, without hesitation.

It was becoming more and more clear to me how much James loved me and how much he was willing to do for me. I began to see, despite being the type of person that always craved to be in control, I was finally learning how to let go of it, even if that meant my bowels.

The following day, seven days after arriving and twenty pounds lighter, I was cleared to go home.

CHAPTER 12

O nce home, I quickly realized the luxury of being surrounded by my own personal comforts was fleeting. James and I had only built our home eighteen months prior, and while doing so, hadn't considered the possible difficulties the layout might present someday, should one of us become incapacitated.

Standing three stories tall, it looked more like a townhouse than a single-family home. There was no basement, meaning the bottom floor was at ground level. We didn't spend much time on the ground floor except to let Gus in and out of the backyard. The middle floor was a large open space for our kitchen, dining, and living rooms. We spent most of our time in this space eating, watching TV, or hosting friends. The top floor housed three bedrooms and two bathrooms.

The prospect of climbing three flights of stairs to get to our bedroom had not seemed an impossible task as we signed our contract. But walking through the garage door after my hospital stay, I immediately felt dizzy. The scene of Gus Gus, from *Cinderella*, faced with a seemingly never-ending staircase to climb and deliver a key to free her from a tower, flashed through my mind.

I expected to be capable of doing most things for myself, considering I was healthy enough to leave the hospital. However, that proved to be incorrect. I constantly needed to rely on James more than I felt I'd relied on my nurses. Simple tasks like readjusting my position in bed, changing my clothes, walking to the bathroom, or even standing in the shower felt impossible without his help.

I began to feel guilty about the amount of time and energy he dedicated to me while also working full time, taking care of Gus, and taking time to do things he needed to do for himself. His physical and mental well-being was an important part of this journey as well. He'd suddenly become a full-time caregiver, and not only was it a job he hadn't applied for, but it was also one I hated to admit needed to be done. I'd never navigated this caliber of physical struggle and had mostly always been able to take care of myself.

Leaving the hospital, I was sent home with a new, yet unwanted fashion accessory. Stitched into my skin, a long rubber tube coiled through my insides, and upon exiting, attached to a transparent soft-ball-sized plastic bulb that resembled a small canteen. Daily, I had to empty out the pink, gunky excess fluid now draining from my abdomen and measure the output.

Besides being gross, it was extremely uncomfortable to be attached to. I had to get creative with the ways I carried it around on my person—in a pocket, safety-pinned to my pants or shirt, even tucked in my sports bra. If not careful, I painfully learned the tube would get caught on doors or drawer handles. I would suddenly feel as though someone was reaching into my stomach and trying to rip out my insides when the tube would snag.

I was elated to find out, a week later, it was time to have this awful souvenir taken out. My sister came into town from California to stay with me for a few days and was able to attend the appointment with me, a choice she later jokingly said she'd regretted. She and James sat at my side in Dr. Zempolich's clinic and watched as she prepared me for what was to come.

"I am just cutting the tube loose. Aren't these cute?" she asked, holding a pair of one-time use scissors. "Here, you can take them home with you." She handed them to me carefully, as if presenting me with a trophy. She gave the tube a small tug, making sure it would not give any resistance. However, my skin had started to heal around it, requiring a little more force.

"Is this going to hurt?" I asked, suddenly aware I was again clenching my entire body in preparation.

"Yes, it is," she said, bluntly. "Try to relax as best you can. On the count of three, take in a deep breath and hold it." I nodded, holding my breath as tightly as I could.

I felt a sudden jolt as she pulled. It didn't budge. Pain seared through my abdomen as we realized the tube hadn't fully disconnected from my abdominal muscle. Already committed to the task at hand, she tugged a second time, even harder, breaking the connection.

This time, the tube broke free and took with it some of my skin. It felt like a long snake slithering through my insides as I watched her continue to pull. To my shock and horror, the final piece to exit my body was a flat silicone filter measuring about two inches wide and eight inches long.

"*That* was in my body?!?" I shouted, relieved it was over and retching in pain.

Having this tube removed was a game-changer. I'd not realized how miserable I'd truly been until I experienced life without it. Not having to carry it around everywhere or empty out the contents multiple times a day was liberating. Not to mention, the site at which it'd exited my body became swollen, itchy, and extremely painful. This was a pivotal moment in my recovery, and I suddenly felt happier and more positive.

About a month after returning home, I felt the best I had through the entire experience. Although not perfect, I knew I wouldn't feel this good once I started chemo in the next few weeks and appreciated what I could get.

One weekend, our friends Zac and Danielle, a couple we are close with, came over to visit and bring me a gift. We'd spent a lot of time together over the years traveling, camping, watching football, and even stood in each other's weddings.

One activity we bonded over was watching the television show *Survivor*. Having seen the show since it began in 2000, I always looked for people who shared in my enthusiasm and fandom. Not to mention, I had a strong desire to go on the show and play the coveted game. It was a regular weekly event in our household to sit in front of the TV and root for our favorite players. Finding other friends who were as passionate about it was the icing on the cake.

Danielle sat beside me on our gray-brown couch and handed me a small teal box, originally used to hold a pack of holiday cards.

"Okay, there is kind of a back story, but go ahead and open it first," she said.

I opened the box and pulled back the tissue paper, revealing a teal buff inside. It wasn't just any buff, but a replica of one worn on the show. The players are divided into tribes and assigned a tribe color, their buff serving as a team uniform worn on their head, arm, or around their neck.

"Oh, I love this!" I said, feeling the soft fabric between my fingers. "I have been looking for things to wear on my head, and we were just looking at buffs the other day!" I held it up so James could see what my excitement had been about.

"And the color is perfect!" he exclaimed.

"It's from *Survivor: Second Chance*, that is even more perfect," I said, unfolding it to reveal the logo and name of the season it represented. The theme of that season was to allow former players to come back and have a shot at redemption—a second chance to win a game that represented so much more than just living on an island for thirty-nine days, trying to win one million dollars. It represented willpower, strength, endurance, self-sacrifice, and above all, what one was capable of when putting their mind and body through hell.

"Open the card," Danielle said, anxiously motioning at the accompanying letter. I'd been distracted trying to remember exactly who'd played that season.

"Okay, did you like, get me on *Survivor*?" I asked, my stomach flipping at the sudden hope she might have pulled something like that off. I opened the card, my interest more than piqued.

It read, "*Hey Jenny, I hear you're over there kicking cancer's butt!*" "You have very nice handwriting," I said, reading the first line.

"It's not mine." My eyes immediately jumped to the bottom of the note to see who'd written the words so nicely printed in front of me. *All the best, Jeff Varner.*

"What the fuck?!?" I exclaimed, my mouth dropping open. My eyes darted back to the beginning, and I read the note from top to bottom silently to myself.

I also hear you're a big Survivor fan. With the challenge you are tackling, I think you're quite the Survivor yourself. So to make it official, I'd like you to have my buff from Second Chance. It's one actually worn on the island in the game—teal to honor your journey. Second chance, to honor your future. If you ever need a dose of positivity, feel free to call me.

"Oh my God! How did you do this?" I asked, realizing the buff in my hand was not a replica, but an original.

"What?!" James asked, not realizing why I'd reacted in such a way.

Danielle explained she'd wanted to give me a teal *Survivor* buff. She knew there'd been one on *Second Chance*. Unable to find a replica online for purchase, she took to a *Survivor* Facebook fan page to ask if anyone knew where she could get one for her friend battling cancer. Another fan took her request to Twitter, tagging several former players, CBS, and Jeff Probst, the show's host.

To her surprise, Jeff Varner, a former player who happened to play on the teal-colored tribe that season, responded. I'd also watched him play the game three different times. Along with his beautifully handwritten card, he sent the buff he'd worn while playing the game, still smelling of sunscreen and bug spray. And, as a final surprise, he gave me his personal cell phone number so I could call and talk to him if I ever wanted to.

James came to my side and read the letter for himself. Both of us were in shock. He leaned over my shoulder as we read it from start to finish a second and third time, continuing to express our surprise at how it'd come to be. James reached for the buff I'd been gripping in my hands, wanting to see, feel, and smell it for himself.

I couldn't believe Jeff had been so generous to part with something I could only imagine was valuable to him, let alone, take the time to write me a note along with it. I was humbled and touched by this wonderfully thoughtful gift my friend, with the help of complete strangers, had given me.

His act of kindness lit a fire inside of me, one I never knew I had—not only to fight like hell to beat this disease so I would live to see another day, but one that made me want to fight so I could one day join the *Survivor* family and play the game myself... a fire that will not go out until Jeff Probst snuffs it out himself.

CHAPTER 13

F ive weeks after surgery, feeling better every day, my treatment plan was
put in place. I felt lucky to have one of the best cancer hospitals only
thirty minutes away from my house, the Huntsman Cancer Institute. On
March 27, I walked into the clinic to meet my oncologist for the first time.

The waiting room was full, making it hard to find a seat. I was first taken
to the lab for a blood draw and watched intently as the nurse filled several
vials, maneuvering in such a way I didn't even flinch. The results would set a
baseline to which future tests would compare. Also, it was important for the
doctors to know if my platelets and red/white blood counts were in a range
that allowed me to begin treatment without potential complications.

Moments later, James and I were led back into another exam room,
and my oncologist, Dr. Lane, entered shortly after. She looked to be in her
mid-forties, had long black hair and striking blue eyes. She wore a lab coat
and dress that went to her knees, revealing her legs to be fit and tan. *I hope
she wears sunscreen*, I thought, seeing as she was an oncologist.

We spoke only shortly about our journey, as she'd already read through
my chart and spoken to Dr. Zempolich prior to our arrival.

"How are you feeling both physically and emotionally right now?" she
asked, removing her glasses, and leaning in, giving me her full attention.

"I feel good. I mean, all things considered." In my mind, however, I wondered how I was expected to answer that question. I didn't know why, but I wasn't being totally honest in how I felt. Truthfully, I was depressed and feeling sorry for myself that the journey to healing wasn't over, but rather, just beginning. I didn't want to tell her about the days I'd spent lying in bed crying because I didn't feel well enough to do anything else. I didn't have the energy to dive into the emotional ups and downs I'd been experiencing since the day of my diagnosis and how I felt I was already changing as a person. And most of all, I didn't want to admit I was scared I was going to die.

"Well, your labs look good, and if you are up for it, I suggest we start your treatment in five days on April 1." She paused. *Was this just a cruel April Fool's joke?* "Depending on how that goes, we'll plan to do each subsequent infusion every third Wednesday, for a total of six treatments." After agreeing on a time frame, Dr. Lane left the room.

A few moments later, her nurse came in and handed me a binder full of resources. Each tab covered a different topic from side effects and home remedies to names and phone numbers of various caretakers, and a list of emergency contacts. She talked through each page with us, detailing what I might come to expect.

"Because chemo can build in the tips of your fingers and toes, it's common to have numbness which we call neuropathy. Sometimes it goes away, sometimes it can continue after treatment is finished," she said, arriving at the side effects page. "It's also common to get mouth sores and nausea with each treatment. Here are some home remedies." She pointed at a list of various over-the-counter items I could purchase to alleviate any discomfort. James reached out and touched my hand.

Looking at the page in front of me, I began to feel overwhelmed at how many unknown side effects I might incur. My shoulders slumped, the weight of this information taking not only an emotional, but now physical toll.

"If you have bowel issues, we have a saying here called 'mush and push,'" she said.

"Mush and push?" James blurted out, not able to control his amusement and laughter.

"Miralax will help with the mush, and Senna-S will help with the push," she said, ignoring his reaction.

"You'll also lose your hair. There are several places you can buy wigs listed here." She pointed at a small list of wig shops. "However, most women find wigs are hot and itchy, and I personally think the vanity isn't worth it." My posture immediately stiffened as I tried, unsuccessfully, not to take offense to her opinion, one I most certainly hadn't asked for.

Losing my hair was one of the scariest things I would have to face. If I wanted to wear a wig, I should be able to do so without being called vain. Knowing I would be seeing this nurse throughout my treatment and wanting to avoid any future awkwardness, I faked a smile and refrained from telling her I'd recently tried on and purchased three wigs of my own in preparation, not vanity.

"How do you feel, babe?" James asked, a few moments after we'd gotten in the car and started driving home.

"Vain," I said, rolling my eyes.

Two days later, while taking a bath, I ran my fingers through my long brown hair and started to cry. It always made me feel feminine, and I was terrified to lose such an important part of my physical identity.

"What's wrong, Jen? Are you okay?" James asked. He often sat and kept me company while I took a bath.

"I think I want to cut my hair," I said, turning toward him, wiping my eyes. "Like, today." I thought perhaps if I was able to cut it before it started to fall out, I would feel as though it'd been my choice. Not to mention, it seemed less traumatic to see shorter hair falling out versus chunks of shoulder length hair.

Within two hours, I sat in my stylist's chair, a black cape draped around my neck, James by my side. She pulled my hair into two loose ponytails. I wanted James to be the one to cut them, not having the desire to do so myself. I took a deep breath and let my tears fall. He rubbed my leg and began to cry with me.

"Are you sure you want *me* to do this?" James asked. I nodded. "You are going to be great. You *are* great. I love you so much," he said. He leaned in and kissed me. We both looked at my reflection in the mirror. I was trying to be strong, to prove I could handle all the changes coming my way. However, I wasn't sure how I would feel or if I would recognize myself once my hair was gone. I hoped this was just another step in taking back control in a situation where I seemed to be on the losing end.

James placed the scissors right above the first rubber band and waited for me to give him the go-ahead. I blinked, indicating I was ready. I felt him pull on the ponytail to keep it tight followed by the sound of the blades slicing through the thick bunch of hair. It reminded me of when I was a little girl.

I'd had an odd affinity for scissors and cutting, not only my own hair, but my friends' hair, too. On one occasion, while my mom taught piano lessons downstairs, I took a pair of scissors and cut off my best friend's ponytail.

We'd recently learned it customary to make a wish when finding an eyelash on your hand or finger. Not wanting to pull out our own eyelashes, we thought hair would be a good substitute. I was hoping for an infinite amount of good luck when I took her long, neatly tied, blonde hair and sliced through it. Maybe this was karma, and all my good luck had run out.

I was softly jolted back to my reality when I felt the last bit of my hair separating from the rest. I sighed, knowing there was no turning back. This was going to be the start of a new me and it'd only taken a few snips. My hair was never going to be the same.

An hour later, evenly cut, styled, and looking fresh, I got my first glimpse of my new hair. To my surprise, I loved how it turned out. The style was fierce and even made me look a few years younger. I walked away from the salon feeling more at peace with what I was about to lose and knew I'd do everything I could to rock a bald head when the time inevitably came.

CHAPTER 14

T he following Monday, April 1, we woke up early, even though my appointment was not until noon. It was deceivingly cold out, despite a bright, cloudless sky. I knew it was going to be a long day, having previously been told chemo could take five or six hours.

We pulled up to the building and handed our keys to the valet, a complimentary service offered for patients. I was already dealing with anxiety and fear. I didn't need the added stress of finding a parking spot in a crowded structure.

"Do you have any questions for me?" Dr. Lane asked. We were having one final meeting before heading to the infusion room. She was once again wearing a knee-length dress.

I'd asked several questions at our last visit, but realized I'd forgotten to ask a rather important one.

"What is the success rate of this chemo?"

"We are starting you on the highest, most potent dose of chemotherapy drugs possible," she said. "We want to try from the beginning to kill every cancer cell with the most rigorous treatment available. Studies have shown if you are not cancer-free after six rounds of treatment, you will most likely never be cancer-free." I felt all the color drain from my face the moment the words left her mouth. "Did you not know that?" she asked, seeing the fear wash over me.

"No, I didn't," I said, my voice quivering. I could feel my chest tighten at this revelation. I felt blindsided. How was this not something I'd been told of sooner? I immediately thought of how lucky my mom had been to have beaten this disease and remained in remission. Her survival was the only thing keeping me from losing all hope at that moment.

"If we find this regime doesn't cure you, then it becomes a matter of managing the cancer moving forward. You would most likely die from it at some point if this doesn't work. I know it is hard to hear, but I want to be straightforward with you." She finished speaking and crossed her hands in her lap.

I tilted my head back, trying to stop my pooling tears from escaping my eyes. I didn't want to let anyone, not even James, see this newly added crack to my already fractured shell. I looked back at Dr. Lane. This was not what I'd wanted to hear, but the only way I'd find out my fate was to begin treatment.

"I believe you're young and healthy enough to beat this. Not to mention, once your chemo is completed you'll start another treatment plan of daily pills. This medication has proven successful in targeting cancer cells specifically caused by the BRCA 1 mutation," she said.

Dr. Zempolich had mentioned this treatment plan in prior conversations. She'd told me this medication wouldn't be safe for me to take if I was pregnant and that I'd likely be on it for five years. This information had ultimately led me to move forward with my hysterectomy.

After finishing our conversation with Dr. Lane, we made our way to the infusion room. Upon walking in I realized I'd been there before, when I accompanied my mom to one of her treatments. It'd been almost twenty years, and it looked nothing like I remembered, but it felt familiar. The image in my memory of a room full of recliners forming a circle, women sharing stories, reading magazines, and eating popsicles together was not the image I saw before me now.

After getting checked in, we took a tour of the space. There were eight sections each containing six patient pods. The pods were equipped with a leather recliner, a television, and a few chairs for guests. They offered a small amount of privacy, but other patients were visible. They all faced a full-length window running from one end of the room to the other that overlooked the Salt Lake Valley. There was a lead nurse and a backup nurse monitoring the group of pods in each section.

I was led to my pod, 7C. It was the second to last section at the end of the infusion room. I was lucky enough to receive a seat right in front of the large window. I unpacked my bag and made myself as comfortable as one could before starting chemotherapy for the first time. I pulled out my new *Survivor* buff and placed it on my head. It was sure to bring me good luck.

My nurse introduced himself as well as a few others who would be assisting throughout the day. He was kind, attentive, and personable, even making me laugh. Before I knew it, he was placing an IV in my arm.

"We are going to administer a few meds prior to starting the chemo," he said, now holding a few vials, bags of fluid, and oral pills. "Before every infusion, we'll give you a combination of steroids, anti-nausea medications, and antihistamines that can help prevent a negative reaction."

I was also attached to a saline drip that felt cool as the fluid entered and coursed through my body. A few moments after my pre-meds were administered, a man approached us with a cart full of snacks. I chose a granola bar and a Rice Krispies treat, both of which I tore into as soon as he walked away.

Settling in, I looked to my left and saw a man in the pod across from me, accompanied by a guest. Because the infusion room was used for more than just chemo, I didn't know what treatment he was receiving, but could see he was asleep. His guest looked up from the book he read intently and gave me a polite smile and nod before returning to the pages in front of him.

With nothing but time to pass, I pondered what this experience might have been like for my mom. She hadn't talked in much detail about her battle, then or in years to follow. I wondered if she'd been scared or what had kept her feeling strong and capable. I wondered what she thought about or did to pass the time during each infusion. I felt sorry I didn't have a better understanding of what her experience had been. I had so many people supporting me. I couldn't recall what her support system looked like or if she really had one. I felt guilty for being a self-centered teenager and not being more aware of thinking to ask.

It was even more important to me that I continue being open and vulnerable about my journey—maybe because I didn't feel capable of going through this battle alone and I needed the support of those around me or maybe so no one would feel guilt someday about not knowing what I'd gone through. Whatever it was, I hoped I could draw strength from what little I knew of her experience and come out stronger for it.

After about an hour of letting the medications work through my system, feeling a bit drowsy, the nurse approached with a large bag of clear fluid marked with various warning labels adhered to it. It was the first of two chemo medications they would administer. He told me the first medication would take about four hours, and the second, another hour after that.

"Are you ready to get this show on the road?" he asked.

"As ready as I'm going to be," I said, realizing how cliché it sounded.

"Now, I'm not sure if your doctor told you, but once we start this medication, there is a fifty percent chance you will have a reaction to it. If you do, we'll stop the drip, flush everything out with saline and start it over at a slower rate," he explained. Dr. Lane had not told me about this possibility, and I immediately became nervous about how my body might respond. He continued, "If you feel anything—shortness of breath, itching, dizziness—please get my attention right away."

Before I knew it, my first round of chemo was hooked up and running through the IV. I was shocked at how easy the whole process had been to that point. For some reason I'd always envisioned chemo as a thick, glue-like substance that would be slow and painful. Even having been there when my mom had an infusion, I didn't remember what it looked like. But it was nothing like how I'd envisioned it in my mind. It was like water, albeit poisonous water.

A woman who worked for the hospital came to my pod just as my infusion started. She asked if I wanted to be a part of a study that would potentially offer insights into the effects of various chemotherapy drugs. She sat next to James in one of my visitor chairs at the foot of my recliner, clipboard in hand, and began asking a few questions.

About five minutes into our conversation, I noticed a few bug bitelike bumps on my stomach beginning to itch. Lifting my shirt to look at them, I felt my heart starting to race. Was I just imagining this and causing myself to get worked up or was something wrong? My heart rate was followed quickly by a rush of dizziness and nausea. I returned my recliner to a fully seated position and reached for James.

"My heart is racing, and I feel like I'm about to throw up," I said, grasping his hand. "I think I might pass out." I fought to keep my eyes open as the room grew dark around me. I worried if I closed them, I would slump over and lose consciousness. I heard my heart rate monitor beeping much faster in the background and felt myself start to get sweaty and hot. "I can't breathe. I need air. I need to take my shirt off," I exclaimed urgently as James rushed to get my nurse. I sat as still as I could to avoid falling out of my seat or vomiting all over myself. The girl conducting the study was now frantically trying to help me stay conscious.

"I feel like I'm going to pee my pants. Someone get me something to pee into, I don't think I can hold it!" I shouted, aware I was feeling so many different things at once, not sure which thing to focus on. The nurse rushed to my pod and immediately stopped the chemo drip and replaced it with saline solution. He also gave me Benadryl to help with any other allergy I might be experiencing from the medications.

"I need you to focus on your breathing. Long, deep breaths in and out," he said, now kneeling at my side, looking directly into my eyes. My vision was still blurred, but I could hear him breathing with me. *Oh my God. I am going to die of cancer.* I drew in a deep breath. *I am going to die. My body is rejecting the chemo.* I breathed out. *Oh my God. I don't want to die from this.* Another deep breath in. *Why is my body doing this?*

I exhaled and started to cry. These thoughts kept racing through my mind, leaving me certain I wouldn't be able to continue my treatment as planned to kill all the cancer in my body, and ultimately, I wouldn't survive.

My heart rate didn't normalize, and before I knew it, a cardiologist and three more nurses were trying to take off my shirt to complete an electrocardiogram or EKG. The task proved difficult because it was soaking wet and sticking to my skin. Beads of sweat dripped from my forehead onto my chest as I slumped over.

"James, can you wipe my forehead for me?" I asked, barely able to speak, handing him my buff I'd just ripped off my head. "I still feel like I'm going to pee my pants, please help me!"

My nurse came back to my pod, now carrying a portable curtain that propped up to give me privacy. I looked around and briefly saw the look of grief and pity on the face of the guest in my neighboring pod. I knew he could hear and see how scared I was, and I could tell he felt badly for me, with just one fleeting look.

The nurse injected an anti-anxiety medication called Ativan into my IV. Within a matter of moments, between the Ativan, the chemo being stopped, and the breathing, I started to feel myself calming down. My heart rate was still high and my breathing labored, but my vision was coming back to me, the sweat no longer dripped, and I didn't feel like I was going to vomit or pee my pants. James helped keep me steady, and I was able to relax little by little.

Fifteen minutes later, after experiencing one of the most terrifying, dark, discouraging and physically tolling moments of my life, I was back to feeling normal—exhausted, but normal. My cardiologist was no longer afraid I would go into cardiac arrest after seeing the results of my EKG. James walked slowly with me and my IV bag, hooked to a portable stand, to the bathroom.

After emptying my bladder, I was able to get the first glimpse of myself in the mirror. My skin was pale gray, all the color having drained and not yet fully returned. However, that wasn't the most alarming thing I noticed. I leaned in closer to get a better look at my eyes. They were completely bloodshot. And not just a light pink color, but a deep crimson red, as if every vein in my eyeballs had exploded. I didn't even recognize myself as I searched the mirror for familiarity.

What I did see was someone who wasn't going to give up, someone who wanted to fight to live to see another day. I stared long and hard at this person, until I was ready to accept this was the journey I was on whether I wanted to be or not. I had a choice to make. Would I feel sorry for myself and let this awful disease take control of me or would I fight like hell to take control of it? I knew the answer. After all, I loved being in control.

Once back in my recliner, the nurse came over to check on me.

"Okay, now we know you are one of the fifty percent who has a reaction to the medication. We are going to start it again, but at half the drip speed this time. Most people who have a reaction the first time don't have another reaction when we start it at a slower speed," he explained.

Knowing I should feel more nervous, but also feeling the Ativan in full effect, I gave an enthusiastic thumbs up.

The nurse started the chemo again, and all we could do was wait. After thirty minutes and no further complication, he increased the drip a little bit more.

James was able to leave to get food, once he felt confident I was in a good place. I could eat, but I was so loopy I didn't even try. His parents came to see me, and I FaceTimed with my mom to tell her what happened...all of which became blurry memories by the end of the evening.

By seven o'clock, seven hours after arriving at the clinic, I was done with my first round of chemo. I knew the road ahead would be difficult, and I'd come to expect the unexpected along the way. However, knowing I was done with my first of six rounds felt monumental. I was on my way up a hill that seemed like a mountain when standing at the base. I was scheduled to return for my next infusion in three weeks.

James packed all my things and helped me walk to the car. I got buckled in and pulled down the visor so I could see if my eyes were still bloodshot. The word *Survivor* displayed back at me; my buff having been placed back on my head. I'd never felt more like a survivor of anything than I did in that moment.

CHAPTER 15

The first two days after my infusion were much better than I'd expected. This was because all the pre-meds they administered would stay in my system for a few days to help combat some of the usual side effects such as nausea, insomnia, muscle aches, and neuropathy, among others.

On day three, and for about four days following, I felt like I'd been hit by a school bus, now those same pre-meds wearing off. Fortunately, I only experienced a small amount of nausea that was easily remedied with Zofran, a common anti-nausea medication I'd taken a few times before. My fingers and toes felt numb and tingly from chemo pooling in the tips. This wasn't a comfortable feeling, but it was something I felt I could live with.

It reminded me of how my hands and feet would feel after a long day playing in the snow as a child. No matter how many pairs of gloves or socks I wore, the cold moisture would always find a way to seep in and leave my extremities numb. Once back in the warmth of my house, thinking hot water would help, I could never seem to thaw them out, and the tingling lasted for hours on end.

I'd been told I would begin to lose my hair sometime between my first and second infusion. To help me feel better, Dr. Lane once told me when it did start falling out it would seem like a lot to me but wouldn't be as noticeable to others. Whether the case or not, at some point it was all going to be gone, no matter how long I may try to avoid it.

The Sunday before my second infusion, I woke feeling rested, having slept through the night, which hadn't been a common occurrence over the last two weeks. This would be the last Sunday in my three-week cycle I would feel as close to normal as possible before beginning all over again. *Maybe James and I could have sex today?* Intimacy hadn't been in the cards since my diagnosis.

James had been awake for an hour or so and was downstairs watching TV. I slowly sat up, letting my eyes adjust to the light peering in through the window. It looked like a beautiful day outside and felt like one inside. My feet found the softness of the carpet, and I stretched my arms and neck, turning my head toward my headboard.

In the corner of my eye, a dark brown object caught my attention, and I jumped out of bed in a panic. *Holy shit! Is that a tarantula on my pillow?* My heart racing, I held back a scream and felt shivers run up my spine. My gaze immediately focused, only to realize the object was not a giant spider, but a pile of my hair that remained on my pillow when I'd sat up. *Oh my God.* I froze, my heart still racing, but now for a completely different reason. No matter how much I'd tried to prepare, the realization hit me that I'd not been anywhere near ready to lose my hair.

I pressed my hand to the back of my head, twirled my hair between my fingers, and gave it a small tug, hoping my little follicles would be strong enough to withstand. I brought my hand in front of me, eyes closed. I breathed out and slowly opened them. Gripped in my hand was a rather large bundle of hair between my fingers, looking frail and broken. I reached back with my other hand and tugged a spot on the left side of my head. Equally as much, if not more, came out.

I pulled a few more times, hoping it would stop after a few tries, but it didn't. I started walking toward the bedroom door, to call for James, and suddenly was thrown off balance. A fist full of hair gripped in one hand, I used my other to steady myself against the mattress. My legs gave out just in time for me to find myself sitting on the leather bench at the foot of the bed. I held the piles of hair in my hands, eventually dropping them into my lap, and cried.

Finally, I mustered enough composure and was able to call out to James and heard him run quickly up the stairs. He entered the room and immediately saw the pile of hair in my lap along with my red, puffy eyes. He kneeled in front of me and put his head to my chest. He started to cry. No words needed to be spoken.

Later that day, after I'd showered and watched as more hair circled the drain, I sat on the couch and watched TV with James. Ten minutes into what we watched, I realized I'd completely zoned out and was impulsively reaching up and pulling out more chunks. My focus only pulled back into view when I heard James say, "Jen, stop doing that!"

It reminded me of the time I sat with my mom on her bed, watching her pull out pieces of hair. I'd felt sorry for her, thinking she could only be experiencing sadness and defeat. However, sitting in my living room doing the same thing, years later, sadness wasn't my strongest emotion and probably hadn't been hers.

Of course, I felt sad, this being the first time it really sank in I had cancer and would now begin to look as though I was sick. But I also felt happy and powerful. This moment was somewhat a "rite of passage" on the journey to healing and someday calling myself a survivor. The chemo was working, doing its job to kill the fast-growing cells, such as hair follicles. I felt I finally understood what that moment meant to my mom as well.

Instinctively, not breaking my gaze with James, I reached back and grabbed another chunk and set it down. "It's kind of fun," I said, the exact words my mom said to me, similarly void of emotion. "Here, you try." James obliged.

The following day, in a show of support, a small group of family and friends gathered in our living room to watch as I shaved James' head and he shaved mine. Sitting in a chair, laughing, and sipping a beer, James was not phased at all by the prospect of being bald, even smiling as I made my first pass down the center of his head. Although his hair wasn't particularly long, the clippers snagged as I tried to make one smooth movement.

"You better not bail on me after this!" he said, jokingly. I could only imagine the bad karma I would receive if I was to back out after he made such a beautiful gesture.

Ten minutes later, after running his hand back and forth over his hairless head, he dusted off the chair and motioned for me to take a seat. "You're going to be beautiful," he said, followed by a kiss on my lips.

He took his place behind me. The buzzing of the clippers grew louder as they came closer to my head. My foot began to shake beneath me. I breathed in and out slowly. I was ready. I felt cold metal and the vibration of the clippers touch my forehead, slowly, yet evenly, making its way to the nape of my neck. Unless I wanted to live with a reverse Mohawk haircut for the next few days, there was no turning back.

I couldn't bring myself to look anyone in the eyes. Tears fell onto the black cape draped over me and streaked to the floor.

"Jenny, haircut?" my two-year-old niece asked her mom, who was holding her a few feet in front of me. After what felt like an eternity, it was done. For the first time since I was an infant, the pile of hair on the floor was greater than what remained on my head.

Upon getting my first look in the mirror at my new self, I was immediately thankful for two things: my head appeared to have a normal shape, and Gus still recognized me. That was enough for me.

Through the remainder of my treatment, the side effects that most unexpectedly knocked me on my ass were insomnia and muscle aches. I was already a light sleeper and needed a noise machine every night to help drown out distracting sounds. Something as simple as a car driving by or the sound of a bird chirping outside my window would typically wake me. Not to mention, I would tend to fixate on a repetitive sound, like water dripping in the sink, and wouldn't be able to fall back to sleep. James proved, yet again, he was an accommodating man when he accepted the noise machine as a non-negotiable in our married life. In fact, he came to require it himself over time.

Following an infusion, it was common for me to remain wide awake at all hours of the night, as if I'd consumed three cups of coffee right before bedtime. Lying in bed, I forced my eyes closed, hoping for sleep to come, and when it wouldn't, I couldn't help but sneak a glance at the time. *It's only been ONE minute?* It didn't help we had a clock that projected the time onto the ceiling, which normally was rather helpful in the middle of the night but was now becoming an obsession to look at. As a result of my inability to sleep, I was left with nothing but my thoughts. I couldn't turn my mind off and would venture down endless rabbit holes, not unlike Alice in *Alice's Adventures in Wonderland.*

Morbid thoughts about mortality and how I would most likely die from cancer reeled through my mind. I wondered if James would get remarried and have a greater love with his new wife. I envisioned what my last moments would be like and who would be at my side to help me leave behind the life being cut too short.

There were even times I wished, for only a few fleeting moments, it was James who was sick and not me. The sound of him softly snoring in bed next to me sometimes caused me to feel irrationally angry. How could he possibly sleep when I was wide awake next to him watching the seconds tick by? I wanted to reach over and shove him out of the bed so he would suffer with me. It felt unfair I had to go through the restlessness alone, even knowing everything James was already sacrificing to take care of me.

In addition to not being able to fall asleep, I experienced body aches I'd never felt before, specifically in my legs. I'd known what shin splints and "growing pains," as my mom called them, felt like. These new aches felt as if my bones were rotting from the inside, and the pain radiated through every inch of my body.

I couldn't stay in one position for too long or the pain would become unbearable. However, not *actually* wanting to wake James, I'd remain as still as possible through the agony, to avoid disrupting him. It was also rather difficult to sleep on my side, due to the healing incision on my stomach. Sleeping on my back, which was always difficult for me, was my only option.

Every night, I went to bed with three or four hot rice bags draped over my legs as well as a heating pad dialed to the highest setting, to help ease the aching. As a last resort, which I often turned to, I'd draw a hot bath in our spare bathroom, at two or three in the morning. This method seemed to be one of the only ways to find the longest-lasting relief, and it wasn't uncommon for me to do this several times in a day.

The leg aches didn't only affect me in the evening, but while I was awake as well. I'd try standing, and the pain was so intense my knees would buckle, causing me to lose balance. Once, slowly making my way down the stairs, pain shot through my body like a bolt of lightning. I missed the step in front of me and fell forward onto the landing. Gus, frightened by my sudden movement, began barking loudly and rushed to my side as I collapsed on the floor and cried.

When initially faced with these side effects, I wasn't sure how long this insurmountable pain would last. With future infusions looming, I worried I wouldn't find relief before putting my body through it all over again. However, the pattern I experienced after each treatment became predictable—feel good for two days, feel like shit for five, and feel almost completely back to normal for the following two weeks.

The ability to mentally prepare myself for those few days of hell became one of the most important practices of my survival. "Mind over matter" is something I'd heard before but never been required to put to the test. However, I learned the mind is one of the most powerful tools we as humans have.

CHAPTER 16

No one prepared me for what fighting cancer would look or feel like. My doctors gave some insight into what to expect, but I knew recovery was different for every person based on many factors. During my treatment, I made it a point not to seek answers on the internet. I'd made the mistake, on a few occasions, of using Google to search for survival rates and statistics, only to become overwhelmed with information, both good and bad. One resource would strongly suggest I had little chance to live, and another said I'd be able to make a full recovery. I didn't know which to trust, although, I was more inclined to believe the worst.

I decided my journey through beating cancer was unique and mine alone. I channeled my energy into focusing on how I could get through each day, sometimes minute by minute, rather than what some website told me to expect. Instead of allowing myself to dread the days of discomfort, I leaned in to accepting the pain, knowing it wouldn't last forever and trusting my body to get through it.

I'd sit in the bathtub and focus on how good the warmth of the water felt on my skin, instead of the pain in my legs. I sat on the couch petting Gus and focused on how his hair felt against my hand rather than my pounding headache. I played the piano, singing along and focusing on the feel of the keys under my fingers, to avoid thinking of how poorly I might sleep that evening. All these techniques helped pass the time that otherwise could be spent focusing on my frailness.

I was surprised the physical toll being taken on my body was solely due to chemo and had relatively nothing to do with parts of my body having been removed. Because I'd never seen or felt my ovaries and uterus, I didn't notice much when they were gone. The loss of them weighed heavily on me in other ways.

The emotional suffering was just as, if not more, exhausting. I'd tried my hardest in the beginning to not linger in negative or self-pitying thoughts. Allowing myself to fall into the pits of depression or anger left me feeling guilty, not to mention weak. After all, I was alive and had it better than some. I didn't want to burden anyone with the weight of what I was going through, so I tried to hide the darkness I often felt.

I answered every call I received, even when I didn't feel like talking. I felt the need to overcompensate for others when they seemed uncomfortable or didn't know what to say.

Commonly, people would minimize their own problems because they were not as difficult as cancer. "Listen to me going on about something so trivial. You have cancer, let's talk about that."

I didn't always need my cancer to be the main topic of conversation. I wanted to be able to talk about the normal day-to-day things people were going through. Cancer or no cancer, being stuck in traffic or having a shitty day at work was still the reality many lived, and my sickness didn't negate that.

My anger and depression would build inside of me, a volcano ready to explode, and I often allowed it to erupt when James merely tried to help. "What are you feeling, Jen? What can I do?" he'd ask, watching me strain to find a comfortable position in bed or after a discouraged sigh.

"You already asked me! I feel the exact same as I did yesterday, I feel like shit. There is nothing you can do. Please stop asking and just let me sulk!"

I began to hate myself for taking my anger out on James. It was not only disrespectful and hurtful, but it was damaging to our relationship. I couldn't explain why I was so intent on hiding my anger and depression from others but letting it come out at his expense.

One evening, feeling good enough to get out of the house, James and I waited to be seated at one of our favorite brew pubs. I felt a small tap on my shoulder and quickly turned to see a friend I'd not seen since before my surgery.

"Jenny! How are you? I'm so happy to see you out and about," she said. I was happy to see her, but also wasn't feeling particularly social. After a moment of chit-chat, I could sense she wasn't sure how to broach the topic of my treatment. Whether because I was giving off an unapproachable vibe or because she wasn't sure what she should or shouldn't say, it felt a little awkward. "You look so skinny!" *That's what you're going with?*

"Yeah, I've lost about twenty-five pounds between surgery and chemo."

"Wow, sounds like I need to get cancer to lose some weight, too!" she said, excitedly.

I blinked in confusion and surprise as I processed what I'd just heard. Part of me wanted to laugh it off and give her the benefit of the doubt. She, like many others I'd encountered, just didn't know how to handle discussing my cancer. However, the emotional toll of trying to compensate for others' discomfort was too much. This was not the first person to say or do something completely insensitive—the x-ray tech who asked if I could be pregnant, the nurse who implied buying a wig was vain.

"Actually, I'd choose to gain fifty pounds rather than go through this fucking nightmare. I'd never wish cancer on myself or anyone else. Never." I hadn't wanted to let her see my angry, bitter side, nor see my eyes filling with tears at the insensitivity of her comment. Yet, I felt relieved when the words came out. My volcano erupted on someone other than James for once. I knew I could no longer shove my real emotions down out of fear they might burden others.

I finally accepted it was okay to be upset, angry, resentful, and even ask why this was happening to me. I felt relieved of the guilt and weakness those thoughts once inspired and started to feel empowered by this new mindset. I'd let everyone see the dark moments as well as the light.

I started to show myself compassion and empathy regarding how I was feeling. If I felt sorry for myself, became depressed, or mad about my circumstance, I'd stay in that moment, rather than try to avoid it. I acknowledged how difficult battling cancer was and that I didn't always feel I was going to make it out alive. I let myself sob, whether I was alone or surrounded by people. I stopped answering every phone call or accepting every visit when I didn't feel up to talking to or seeing someone.

I leaned into the reality of my situation, rather than pretend everything was okay. In doing so, I began to feel more control than I had in over a year, since beginning our fertility journey. I knew the difficult moments would still come, but I didn't let them overstay their welcome. I would pick myself off the floor, wipe away the tears, and forge ahead.

Each of my infusions got easier to handle. Not to mention, the time seemed to be going a lot faster than in the beginning. I lived in threeweek increments, starting the cycle over each time. Despite the hardships I faced, there were also beautiful, memorable moments along the way.

One June morning, fifteen of my friends, family, and colleagues gathered to show support by walking a 5k race with me, the proceeds being put toward cancer research. I celebrated my thirty-fifth birthday, the day after an infusion, with dinner at one of our favorite local Italian restaurants in Salt Lake City.

My wedding photographer reached out and asked if she could take photos to document my journey. She arranged for a makeup artist and florist to help make the occasion special. The final images were a stunning tribute to the different stages of acceptance and grief I'd experienced in such a short amount of time. Being able to feel feminine and beautiful as well as raw and emotional simultaneously was one of the most therapeutic experiences I could have asked for.

In July, the weekend before my final infusion, I checked off a bucket list item. James and I, along with a few other family members, went out to Los Angeles (L.A.) to attend the last show of Paul McCartney's tour, which ended with Ringo Starr coming out on stage to play a few songs. This moment had the entire crowd on their feet, screaming with shock and uncontrollable excitement.

While in L.A., we visited a restaurant and bar made famous by a reality show I loved, *Vanderpump Rules*. The bar, Tom Tom, named after two cast members, had recently opened. The line to get in was long and filled with other fans, wanting their chance to snap a photo, not unlike me. We'd been lucky enough to make a reservation.

It felt like the red carpet had been rolled out as I walked to the front of the line. And as I did, both Toms were standing near the door. Feeling confident from the liquid courage I'd partaken at dinner, I walked up to them and asked for a picture.

"I would really appreciate it," I said, "I have cancer." Sometimes I shamelessly resorted to pulling the cancer card. This time, it got me a kiss on top of my bald head and a free shot with them. It was totally worth it.

Three days after our trip, on Wednesday, July 17, I was back in an exam room at the Huntsman Cancer Institute, while Dr. Lane looked over the results of my blood draw. All my numbers were in normal range, and I was cleared to begin my sixth and final infusion. During the physical exam, checking for any unusual pain or signs of concern, she and I laughed and cried together. I knew I'd continue to see her in the months and years to come, but I was happy, relieved, and emotional while recalling the moments we'd shared together.

Prior to leaving the room, we embraced. I felt as though in that moment, my body released all the stress and fear I'd been holding for eighteen weeks. In its place, I felt a calm resolve overcome me. I knew everything was going to be okay. I'd fought a valiant and difficult fight and survived. And with that wonderful feeling, I entered the infusion room, ready to put cancer behind me.

Something was different as I settled into my pod. I didn't feel the same dread of what the next few days would hold. And though I'd not had a negative reaction to the chemo since my first infusion, I suddenly didn't care if anything happened, knowing it would be the last time I'd ever have to sit in that chair.

Nearly an hour after arriving, my chemo had been started and was searching for any last signs of deadly cells lingering in my body. They could try as hard as they wanted to hang on, but they weren't going to survive. I took two Rice Krispies treats from the snack cart, because today was a special day. A dose of Ativan helped me to relax and coast restfully through my five-hour infusion.

My sister, brother, and in-laws were able to come into my pod at various times to visit, helping the time pass by. In moments, I thought about where I'd started and how lucky I was I'd been able to complete my various infusions without complication, something I momentarily thought impossible after my allergic reaction on my first round.

I looked at the last bag of fluid dripping into my IV and thought how our little EmbryLowe patiently waited in a freezer to be brought into the world. My resolve to keep fighting had been to one day hold my sweet baby in my arms. I couldn't help but smile.

The bag emptied, and my treatment was complete. James leaned down and pressed his forehead into mine. "Babe, you are *done*!" he said, his tears now falling onto my lap.

I gathered my things, feeling overwhelmed and sluggish. I looked around at the people still receiving treatment and wondered where life would take them or how many more times they'd need to come back to this place.

I wondered how they might feel when they heard me ring the gong, a celebratory ritual every cancer patient got to do after their last chemo. I hoped that hearing the sound would empower them to keep fighting so they could similarly ring it someday. I smiled as I walked past a few occupied pods, proud of what I'd just conquered.

Outside the waiting room were twelve of my loved ones, eager to congratulate me and celebrate my victory. They all stood around a table where a large gong sat. Next to it was a certificate of completion and a white 16 × 20 picture frame James had gotten for me. Inside was a simple printout of a teal ribbon above the word "Survivor." Attached to the frame was a small mallet James had also purchased that I would use to ring the gong and take home as a keepsake.

I hugged each family member, softly sniffling at the start and end of each hug. Something I'd never considered when faced with losing my hair was how important the tiny ones inside my nose were. Unbeknownst to me, they kept it from running like a leaky faucet. Since beginning chemo, I sniffled uncontrollably, day in and day out, trying to save tiny droplets of snot from awkwardly falling out. If I hadn't looked sick, I'd assume people thought I had a cocaine addiction.

I walked over to the table and picked up the mallet. I'd been waiting for this moment since the day I'd found out I had cancer. I turned to face the group.

"Thank you so much for being here and thank you so much for everything you've done for our family. I don't think we could've done this at all without you. And James," I said, looking directly at him. I knew there were not any words I could speak to express my gratitude to him. "Your love and support have kept me breathing, living, and fighting. You saved my life, and I wouldn't be here if it weren't for you." It was simple but true. He made me feel capable and strong in the moments I would've slumped into the grip of defeat. I hugged and kissed him, then turned back to face the gong.

I stood still, staring at this symbol in front of me, anticipating how it would feel and how it would sound. I'd heard it a few times from my pod during an infusion, followed by claps and shouts of joy. I wanted to remember every moment of this. Every tear shed, every moment of hopelessness, and every ounce of discomfort I'd experienced began to boil to the surface. I started to cry, gripping the mallet tightly in my right hand. I imagined my cancer as an object I needed to physically assault to ensure it wouldn't try to fuck with me again.

"One," I breathed in deeply, "two," deep breath out, "THREE!" My mallet crashed into the brass target with force. The vibration felt like a small explosion in my hand. I hoped everyone in the hospital heard the sound and knew what it meant. Cancer was no longer welcome in my body, and I wanted everyone to know it. Claps erupted from not only my small group but also from behind me, inside the infusion center. Relief washed over me, along with the biggest smile I'd ever worn. Goosebumps ran up my arms, meeting at the back of my neck.

I no longer had ovarian cancer.

CHAPTER 17

S hortly after I started chemo, while I physically battled a life-threatening disease, I always reminded myself of what led us down this path. If James and I hadn't been trying to start our family, we wouldn't have gone through IVF, and therefore, would not have found my cancer in time, if at all. The desire to become a mother and creating EmbryLowe literally saved my life.

Each day I struggled was another day I fought for the life of my unborn child. I was eager to know how EmbryLowe would come into the world, and some of my friends and family thought it a dangerous question to contemplate. I was still undergoing treatment and not able to know if I'd ever be cancer-free. However, thinking about our next steps gave me bits of hope to hold onto in moments of darkness. I saw fragments of light when I thought of how beautiful our first encounter with our sweet little baby would finally be. But I had no idea what the journey post-cancer would look like, as if it hadn't already been complicated enough, and I was intimidated by the unknown.

It hadn't even been one-year since walking into Dr. Barney's office, hoping to find answers and, ultimately, losing my ability to carry my own child. A lot had happened in a short amount of time, and I didn't know how to allow myself to properly mourn. I wasn't certain I'd even accepted it yet.

What I did know was bringing EmbryLowe into our lives would have to be done via surrogacy. I understood it meant watching another woman pregnant with my child. Before I could fathom what the experience might look like physically or emotionally, I had to admit finding someone willing or able to do it might be difficult.

My knowledge about surrogacy was limited. In truth, it came mostly from reading about celebrities paying thousands of dollars for other women to carry their babies. I was afraid the option might be out of reach for us financially.

In late April, only having been through two rounds of chemo, I decided to take to Facebook to ask if there was anyone in my world with information to help me know where to begin.

As James and I have been moving forward with my cancer treatment, we are very much still mindful of what led us to this point in the first place. Trying to start a family. It might seem too soon to be having this conversation, but I think it will help us hold on to hope for what greatness is to come after I am cancer-free.

With our little EmbryLowe waiting patiently to come into this world, we will be forced to investigate and research surrogacy options. We have very little knowledge about this process. As we went through fertility treatments, we found so many willing to share their stories with us by sharing ours. So, now we ask again, that others help by sharing their stories.

We would love to know if any of our friends have had experience with surrogacy whether through an agency or through personal relationships. We would love any advice on how to move through this process to find the right person to carry our baby. Maybe someone knows the best agency, or someone knows someone that has been and loves to be a surrogate. We would just love to hear from you. Please feel free to DM me to keep things private if you want. But any help or advice would be greatly appreciated.

Later that night, I received a text from my sister-in-law, Allison. She and my brother, Mike, had been married for nineteen years and had four children of their own, having made me an aunt for the first time. All her pregnancies had been complication-free, and they knew they were done having kids of their own.

I would totally do it. And to be honest, the thought has been going through my mind this week. I didn't say anything because it seemed a little presumptuous. That is...if you think a forty-one-year-old woman is a good option!

We appreciated her offer, but weren't sure how serious she was, and worried about the types of complications that could arise from a family member carrying our baby. If it's advised to not mix family and business, I didn't know what would be said about mixing family with creating a life.

The following week, I scheduled a meeting with a new fertility clinic known for specializing in surrogacy. During this thirty-minute consultation, a lot of information was unpacked in detail.

We sat in an ironically sterile-looking office, across from our designated surrogacy liaison, Melissa. She started by asking if we planned to use our own eggs/embryos or those from a donor. This was important in determining if we'd need a "traditional surrogate" or a "gestational carrier."

I'd been unaware there were multiple terms to describe surrogacy, but learned a traditional surrogate is someone who donates her eggs and subsequently carries the baby. A gestational carrier, or GC, is a woman with no biological or genetic relation to the child she carries. A flash of anxiety came over me. If I'd felt uninformed during my fertility journey, I was suddenly aware of how much deeper my ignorance would go in relation to surrogacy.

Melissa slid a few brochures across the table and talked us through each one. She informed us the clinic didn't have a formal database of potential GCs but regularly worked with women who'd been medically cleared to be one. When a couple was seeking a GC, they'd be put on a waitlist, and once at the top of that list, the clinic would put the two parties in touch. From there, it worked much like a job interview. Both parties would meet and decide if they were a good fit for each other.

We were also told to consider the cost of going this route, as it could impact the person we chose. The compensation for a GC to merely carry a baby, not including medical costs or other various expenses associated with pregnancy, could range anywhere between $30,000 to $100,000. Several factors determined how much a GC could charge including if the woman was a first-time GC, had successfully been one before, or if her medical insurance covered surrogacy.

To my surprise, another popular option was asking a friend or family member. This could potentially ease the financial burden, as most family or friends wouldn't be looking for monetary gain. It also offers a more connected and special experience for everyone involved. However, as wonderful as this prospect sounded, I continued to grapple with asking someone I knew to make such a huge physical sacrifice.

Regardless of the path we chose in finding our GC, we knew she'd have to be over twenty-one years old and previously given birth to at least one healthy baby. This not only proved she could carry a baby without complications, but also meant she had a firsthand understanding of medical risks pregnancy posed.

Once we found a GC who met the initial requirements, both parties would undergo a psychological screening by a mental health professional. It was necessary everyone understood not only the physical but also the emotional toll surrogacy could have on an individual as well as a couple.

Additionally, legal counsel would be obtained to assist in creating a contract outlining the terms of the surrogacy. Within a week, despite not yet knowing who our GC was, James and I arrived at a consultation meeting with the attorney we'd selected.

After making introductions, we found ourselves quickly engaged in conversation about his history in reproductive law. He was knowledgeable about Utah's intricate and sensitive surrogacy regulations and explained the steps of the legal process to us in detail.

Knowing everything needed to select and move forward with a GC, I was once more being reminded of how little infertility, and all that comes with it, are publicly talked about. Not to mention, how anyone was able to afford it. It began to make sense to me why surrogacy seemed an elitist solution to a common problem.

A few days later, while talking to my brother on the phone, I described some of the difficulties and frustrations we'd been feeling about the process. Later that evening, I received another text from Allison.

I hope you know my offer still stands... as far as my uterus goes. There are pros and cons, and it would be something to discuss for sure if you're interested. But just so you know, I'm open to talk and investigate the possibility. I don't know if my age disqualifies me but I am willing to find out. No pressure because I won't be offended if you don't use me. But I want you to know I am willing.

Sitting on the same couch where I'd been gifted my *Survivor* buff, I was again left speechless. I turned to James and read the text aloud.

"Is she serious?" he asked. Before he could even finish his question, I was pushing the "call" button on my phone.

"Hello?" she answered.

"Are you serious?" I blurted out, not even one hundred percent certain it was her.

"Yes! I mean, I think so," she said, laughing. "I haven't really talked to Mike about it in much detail, but if I was a viable candidate, and it made sense, then yes."

We both sat in silence. I tried to gain my composure and allow this beautiful moment to simmer. Not only was I shocked at the generosity of someone I knew so well, but it was the first time since we began our journey I heard "yes." So many times over the previous year we felt we'd been thrown down, kicked, and beaten bloody. I'd forgotten what it felt like to hear something positive. Her offer was the spark to my match I'd thought would never light again.

A few days later the four of us sat across from one another in our living room. Gus forced his way in between them, which he often did when guests came over. His head rested on Mike's lap and his back end on Allison's. I felt a flutter in my stomach. I was more anxious and nervous than I'd expected, realizing I didn't know how to start the conversation. I was struck by how comfortable we felt, nonetheless.

Something made me believe if we'd been meeting a stranger for the first time, we'd have been dressed to impress and on our best behavior. This was more casual, like a typical Sunday family dinner gathering... minus the fact we were there to have a conversation that could potentially change all our lives.

"For a while now, I've had this feeling, even though I knew I was done growing my own family, I wasn't done growing *our* family as a whole, if that makes sense," Allison said, being the first to break the silence. "I didn't really understand why or how I could feel that way until you found out about your cancer. I wondered if it meant I was supposed to somehow help you and James." Her eyes filled with tears. I reached over and pulled a few tissues out of a box sitting on our side table. Handing her one, she began to dab at her eyes.

"When you made your post on Facebook about EmbryLowe, I was overcome with a strong feeling this was how I was meant to help grow our family," she said, choking up. Mike put his hand on her leg and continued looking in our direction. "I was just completely heartbroken for you when you learned you couldn't have your own children. It isn't fair that something so beautiful and amazing has been taken from you." I was touched by her emotion regarding my becoming a mother.

"All of this to say, I want to help the two of you and find out if or how I could be your surrogate."

James and I were both deeply touched by her offer, as well as my brother's support. We acknowledged this would be a sacrifice made by both as well as one they needed to agree on together. There would be ups and downs with this responsibility including enduring another pregnancy. However, having seen them grow as a couple over the years, I knew they wouldn't make an offer like this lightly and trusted they'd contemplated the pros and cons. If any couple was up for the task, I was confident in their ability.

Growing up, Mike and I hadn't been particularly close. Nine years my senior, our age gap was just big enough we didn't have much in common. However, as we got older, our age became less a factor, and we grew close. Maybe because our other two siblings moved to California and we both remained in Utah, or, by complete coincidence, our career paths led us to working together in the same department of the same financial institution. I felt we'd created a special bond in our adulthood.

In preparation for our discussion, I'd found some commonly asked questions for potential GCs online. They were printed out in front of me, marked with highlighter and scribbles in the margin. We knew there might be topics difficult to discuss and wanted to be sure we'd come to some agreements before feeling confident to move forward.

"Who is your doctor and how do you feel about us being present at appointments or even in the delivery room?" I asked, reading the first set of questions on my list.

Allison agreed James and I should attend any appointments as well as both be present during the birth. I'd worried initially that the idea of James and I seeing such an intimate side of Allison would possibly cause discomfort or feelings of awkwardness. However, I was pleasantly and thankfully surprised when this issue did not present itself as a deal-breaker.

"I hope you both know how much that means to us," James said. "I'd never want either of you to feel uncomfortable with being exposed to anything otherwise meant to remain private between the two of you. And if that means I'm not as involved, I would completely understand."

"That is considerate of you," Mike said, a comforting smile on his face. "But we truly want you both to experience this as authentically as possible, and we understand what that entails."

As we continued, the topics became a bit heavier in tone. Specifically, around the possibility of becoming pregnant with multiples and under what circumstances we would agree, if at all, selective termination was an option.

"Well, here's where things get a bit tricky," I said, smiling awkwardly. This was the part of the conversation I felt could make or break Allison agreeing to do this.

"Even if we knew the baby wasn't fully developing or wouldn't live long after being born, I'd still want to give you those precious moments," Allison said, blinking faster to prevent more tears from welling in her eyes. "For me, knowing what it feels like to hold your child for the first time, even if I knew I only had ten minutes with them, I'd choose to have those ten minutes every single time." We all agreed that Allison's life being endangered was the only acceptable reason to terminate the pregnancy.

After making plans for next steps, I realized how important and necessary it was to maintain honesty, vulnerability, and good communication throughout the entire surrogacy journey. I was fortunate two people I trusted and loved were eager to be involved, making things easier to navigate as well as agreeable.

My heart ached for couples struggling to find someone to help grow their family. I was being offered an incredible gift, one I would never take for granted. And no matter how lucky I felt, I couldn't shake the fear it was too good to be true.

CHAPTER 18

By mid-May, I was still being treated with chemo. Allison and Mike met with Melissa to cover the information she'd presented to James and me not long before. Allison scheduled the exams necessary to be given medical clearance. This included blood work as well as the dreaded water ultrasound I'd endured on my birthday, less than a year prior. Seeing as she'd never experienced issues with any of her pregnancies, I allowed myself to remain cautiously optimistic.

A few days after her exam, my phone vibrated on our coffee table next to the couch. I'd just gotten comfortable, my pillow positioned behind my head, and was watching TV, trying to distract myself from the toll of my recent infusion. Annoyed I had to move, I reached over to see who was calling.

"Hi Jenny," Melissa said on the other end, after I'd scrambled to answer the call. Seeing her name, I quickly moved into a sitting position and accidentally kicked Gus off the couch. "I just wanted to call and let you know we have the results from Allison's exam and everything looked great." I let out a sigh of relief, realizing I'd been holding my breath since answering. "We believe she'd be a great fit for you and James if you'd like to move forward with her!" I was elated by this news and immediately called James to tell him. There was no question in our minds what we wanted to do.

A few months later, after my final treatment in July, I'd started my new, yet less invasive treatment regimen of pill-based chemo. Somehow I'd found energy to continue making progress through each required step on our surrogacy journey. Not to mention, I also went back to work after taking a six-month leave of absence.

I'd now worked as a trust manager for roughly twelve years since graduating with my bachelor's degree in business administration in 2007. While working this job full time, as well as a part-time serving job, I'd also gone back to graduate school to earn a master's in business administration in 2011.

My career had taken me down various paths, helping me gain business experience and grow professionally in several ways. However, I felt I'd reached the peak of my potential and found myself feeling more dread about going back to work than about any of my infusions. That told me something important. Amidst all the chaos, I knew my heart was no longer in the work I'd been dedicated to for more than a decade.

Through my experiences with infertility as well as cancer, I gained a strong desire to enter the world of healthcare. Although I knew I wouldn't become a doctor or nurse, I had seen firsthand how life-changing an illness could be during various interactions I'd had. I wanted to help ease that burden for others, so much so, I quit my job only two weeks after returning to work.

I was offered a new opportunity managing national accounts with one of the largest physician staffing companies in the nation. Although a drastic shift in fields, I felt myself gaining some of the control I'd been so desperately craving.

In Mid-August, James and I were able to meet with the mental health provider completing our psychological evaluation. We knew we'd be discussing our journey to become parents, what kind of support we'd have, and how to handle the loss of control during a pregnancy. However prepared we felt to discuss these topics, we found it hard not to be offended by this requirement in general.

We parked our car outside the bland, brown brick building in downtown Salt Lake City. We entered a small waiting room and filled out what felt like the millionth intake form in the last year. A petite, brown-haired pregnant woman walked through the doorway and called for us. We followed her back to her office, as she waddled to the end of the hall.

"How far along are you?" I asked. I took a seat on the couch directly across from the wingback chair she plopped into.

"Eight months," she responded, out of breath from the walk. She seemed hesitant to say much else about the pregnancy, and I assumed it was out of respect for our circumstance. "Let's get started. Tell me a little about yourselves." She held a pen in her hand, ready to take notes.

"Actually, before we get to that," James said, repositioning himself as he leaned forward, "I want to be candid in telling you I'm rather offended we even have to be here today." I was thankful James was brave enough to say it, not to mention, so kindly.

"I understand it has nothing to do with you, and you're only facilitating a legal obligation," he said. I slowly moved my hand to the middle of his back for support. "However, it's hard not to feel deeply bothered. Everything we've been through, why we're even here, is because of our desire to have a child." Once again, I felt so much love for James. He always said things in a much more elegant, respectful way than I did. He was the yin to my yang and made up for my inability to know how to express myself in uncomfortable situations.

"Adding to that, if I may, I think it's hard to understand why this is necessary considering there are plenty of people who have kids but shouldn't," I said, attempting to keep a similarly respectful tone. "The law doesn't require them to go through any kind of psychological evaluation."

"I completely understand what you're saying, and I agree with you," she said. "I can see how this process can make you feel that way, especially after you have already been through so much. It seems very unfair to be placed in this position," she responded empathetically.

Although expressing our feelings didn't change our requirement to be there, doing so felt therapeutic, and we appreciated her acknowledging our concerns. James and I passed the evaluation as did Mike and Allison.

By mid-October, we were almost prepared for the transfer. We'd agreed upon the contract's final details including a compensation plan everyone felt was fair. Although Mike and Allison weren't helping us to receive monetary gain, James and I still wanted to make monthly payments to help pay for unforeseen costs arising from the pregnancy. It seemed the least we could do seeing they were saving us from paying the standard GC fee of $30,000.

Allison underwent one last physical evaluation called a "mock cycle." This entailed preparing her body as if about to complete a transfer, injecting two weeks of daily hormone shots inside the familiar black circles recently drawn on her butt cheeks. However, on the would-be transfer day, she underwent an endometrial receptivity analysis, a genetic test of her endometrial lining. This test would help narrow down the optimal window of time, down to the day and hour that would more likely result in the successful transplant of EmbryLowe. I was again left to marvel at what was scientifically possible.

After Allison's mock cycle, there was one final task we'd need to complete prior to our now scheduled transfer date, November 21. Because we'd changed fertility clinics, James and I would be required to move EmbryLowe to the new facility.

On October 22, 2019, which happened to be our third wedding anniversary, we drove the familiar route to our original clinic to pick up our immeasurably valuable, yet microscopic EmbryLowe. We were led directly back to the sperm rodeo, catching a glimpse of the infamous black leather couch, clean and ready for what, or should I say who, was to come.

"Wanna go in there, for old times' sake?" I asked James, raising my eyebrows scandalously. He laughed and rolled his eyes, clearly not interested in reminiscing.

"In here, you'll see all the containers in which we house samples," the embryologist said, leading us into a large walk-in freezer. Inside were roughly twelve metal tanks appearing to weigh around twenty pounds. "Each tank is filled with liquid nitrogen and holds about ten canisters. Each canister contains samples from thirteen to fourteen patients. Eggs, embryos, semen, you name it, we got it." He led us to the tank where EmbryLowe waited and opened the lid. A cloud, like fog in a haunted house, escaped the confines of the container, evaporating quickly, but not before I felt its coldness on my skin.

The embryologist removed a small, white Styrofoam cup, the kind you drink gas station coffee from, with a long metal straw sticking out. The bottom half of the straw was immersed in liquid nitrogen. I expected a dramatic reveal as he slowly pulled the straw out for us to see.

"Do you see that bubble?" he asked, not able to point meticulously because of the bulky protective gloves he wore. James and I both squinted, leaning forward for a closer look. "Inside that bubble is your embryo." It reminded me of the mosquito trapped inside prehistoric resin on the handle of Dr. Hammond's cane in *Jurassic Park*.

To the side of the large tank was a smaller, less impressive tank, in which we would transport EmbryLowe. He placed the straw back into the cup and set the cup inside the smaller tank, through a wide opening at the top. With a few twists and snaps, the lid was closed. "I'm just going to need you to sign here, and you're set to go," he said, handing me a clipboard. I signed the document indicating we were now in possession and fully responsible for our creation.

"This looks like a Soviet-era milk jug," James said, carrying the heavy tank carefully out to our car. I sat in the passenger seat with my legs spread and the tank placed on the ground between them. Although it'd been small in comparison to the other tanks in the lab, it reached just above my bent knees. I pressed my thighs tightly against it to ensure it didn't move. Even though it looked indestructible, we made the twentytwo-mile drive with our hazards blinking, in the slow lane, never breaking the speed limit. Forty minutes later, we were on our way back home, sans EmbryLowe, who was now safely home in a new canister.

One sunny day in early November, after learning the date of our upcoming transfer, James' sister came over to visit and give us a gift. She handed me a bag with white tissue paper spilling over the top.

An envelope was neatly placed between the handles, which James picked up and opened, revealing a Christmas greeting card inside.

Hi you two!

This may look like a Christmas gift, but it's actually an "I'm so happy you're trying to grow your family" present.

Sometimes I think "Hope" is underrated. Having hope in almost every circumstance only improves it, no matter the outcome. Hope keeps us positive, optimistic, and with an eye open to finding the good. Being hopeful keeps us looking forward, even if difficulty or uncertainty makes us stay where we are for a moment.

I hope beyond hope you two have a baby. I hope this journey you're on ends with the sweetest, most loved, most spoiled little thing this family will ever see! But right now I mostly hope you two can keep hope. In all the hard of this, I hope you have hope in each other, your family, and the love we all have for you. We love you so much!

This gift may be seasonal, but I hope that, no matter the outcome, you can put this out every year and remember this season in your family's story and the hope you had for all that is to come. Because there's only good in store when it comes to you two!

James finished reading the card aloud with a smile. Tears built up in both our eyes, touched by the words his sister wrote. I reached into the bag and in one swift movement, pulled out a twelve-inch by twelveinch gray framed wooden sign. The word "hope" was stamped in red paint in the center of a white background. The sign was simple, but the message was radiant. I immediately knew it would be one of my favorite decorations.

The idea of hope was one that permeated throughout my journey with fertility, both related to survival and now with becoming a mother. Finding hope was not always easy or rational, but it was something intangible I found myself grasping in moments when nothing seemed possible. Keeping that hope was often the only thing leading me to believe something good was to come.

It helped me see the silver linings in moments when all I wanted was to be negative and give up. It changed how I'd perceive and react to trials in the future because without it, I saw how easy it was to be lost in pain and suffering. This gift now gave me a physical reminder to always have hope.

CHAPTER 19

On Thursday, November 21, nearly a month after EmbryLowe's big move, Mike, Allison, James, and I sat together patiently in the clinic's waiting room. Although not how we'd originally envisioned our pathway to parenthood, we finally made it to transfer day. We'd gone through more than our share of speed bumps, and I felt pride for what I'd conquered to get here.

"Are you nervous?" I asked Allison, our fingers interlaced.

"Yes, but they gave me Vicodin, so I feel relaxed."

I spent a moment thinking about the physical sacrifices she'd made and what more it would entail if successful. I squeezed her hand in gratitude.

After a short wait, mostly spent in nervous anticipation, we were all back in the exam room. Allison was now in the position I'd been in all too many times. The room was dimly lit, and soft music played through the speakers.

"Can you believe this is happening? Like, really happening?" Mike asked. "I mean, who'd have thought I'd maybe tell people someday my wife was pregnant, but not with my baby?"

"Even better, she'll be pregnant with your brother-in-law's baby," James quickly added. "And you watched it happen!" We all laughed at how absurd it sounded.

"I just want to thank you two again for making this possible for us," I said after the laughter stopped. My emotions were beginning to build as I realized we were possibly only moments away from making my dreams of becoming a mother more real than they'd ever been. "I love you both, and no matter what happens, this will always be an experience I hold near and dear to my heart."

A knock on the door interrupted the moment, and Dr. Fry entered the room. I'd met him one time prior. He was refreshingly energetic and introduced himself to James, Mike, and Allison, this being his first time meeting them.

"Well, let's get this party started!" he said, clapping his hands together and reaching for the light at the foot of the exam table.

"You're going to want to watch the monitor above the door," he said, pointing to a small screen I hadn't noticed hanging above the entrance. "You'll be able to see the embryo through the lens of a microscope on the screen. It will be pulled into a syringe and brought in here for us to complete the transfer. Any questions?"

At the exact moment he finished talking, a small image on the screen drew our attention. Looking only like a tiny speck of dust at first, the lens zoomed in to allow us a closer view of this beautiful miracle. The tears in my eyes made it hard to see the syringe pulling EmbryLowe in through a tiny needle. After quickly wiping my eyes, the tiny speck of dust was no longer visible.

The nurse brought the syringe and a catheter into the room and handed it to Dr. Fry. The view on the monitor switched to Allison's uterus, which would allow us the ability to watch EmbryLowe's journey.

"I'm inserting the catheter. You can see it there." He pointed to the moving image. "Perfect, just where I need it. Are you ready?" he asked Allison, and we all answered.

We watched the tiny little bubble surrounding EmbryLowe make its way through the catheter, coming to rest in Allison's uterus. "Done!" he exclaimed. I felt my entire body relax, not realizing how tightly I'd been squeezing every muscle.

"I know this is your only hope, so I'm sending all the positive, implanting vibes I can possibly muster," Dr. Fry said, unaware of how his choice of the word "hope" sent a shock wave through my body. After leaning the table back, his job was done. We were now left to anxiously wait for fourteen days to see if the transfer worked.

The next two weeks were much like the times we'd waited between each of our IUI's. It helped that Thanksgiving fell one week after the transfer, providing distraction with one of our favorite holidays. While sitting around the table with James' family, I was in a different place both physically and emotionally than I'd been the year prior. I'd lost my ability to have children, survived a life-threatening disease, and was one week away from finding out if EmbryLowe would be joining us the following year.

I'd always had things in my life to be thankful for, but this Thanksgiving took on a different meaning. I didn't feel sad or scared about the future like I had. I didn't feel the need to curl up on the bed and cry about the hardships I faced. I'd proven I could overcome more than I'd ever imagined I was capable. I was thankful to be alive and married to a man who'd sacrificed so much of himself to help ensure I'd be able to celebrate this holiday and many more to come.

On December 2, two weeks after the transfer, Allison had a blood test to determine if she was pregnant. Melissa told us the results could take a few hours and to expect a call around five o'clock. James and I ensured we could be together when the call came through, and I'd even asked Melissa to leave a message as a precaution.

"What are you feeling?" I asked James. Both working from home, we sat across from one another at the dining room table. I'd noticed him staring off, obviously contemplating the news to come.

"I'm just nervous. This call will drastically send our lives in one direction or another." He shook his head as if it would lessen the disbelief we'd finally arrived at this crossroads.

At 12:55 p.m., my phone rang as I finished an urgent work task. Not thinking Melissa would be calling at this hour, I let it ring three times before I looked to see her name.

"Holy shit, babe! She's calling right now!" I said, holding the phone for him to see, my heart racing. I stared at the screen hoping she hadn't called by mistake, waiting for the voicemail notification to pop up.

After what felt like ten minutes, I heard the chime indicating I had a new unheard message.

James and I found our place on the couch next to one another and held hands. The gravity of this moment began pulling us into an excited panic.

"Before we listen, I just want you to know how much I love you, Jen," James said, his palm sweaty in mine. "I'm so proud of you for all you've done to make today possible, and no matter what happens, I'll always be by your side." He took a deep breath. "Are you ready?"

"I love you, too, babe, so much," was all I could say, my thumb hovering over the "play" button.

"*Hi Jenny, this is Melissa. So Allison's HCG number is 276. We want to see a number at least one hundred or above for a positive pregnancy test. So, congratulations, this is an excellent start. Her estrogen and progesterone are right on track so she's gonna continue all of her meds, and then we'll retest again in one week. So, excellent, excellent news. Congratulations. Call me if you want to talk, and let me know when I can call Allison. Thanks!*"

We hadn't even heard the entire message before breaking down in tears. After we heard the number was 276 and only needed to be higher than one hundred, nothing else mattered. We were FINALLY pregnant. Nothing could ruin this moment we'd waited two years for. We'd fought like hell through all the physical and emotional struggles, and we deserved this moment more than ever.

All there was to do was hug each other and cry. We shed tears of happiness, tears of relief, tears of worry, even tears of sadness at what we'd lost along the way. Every ounce of feeling expressed or bottled up in the last two years was now leaving our bodies through our eyes.

"Let's listen to it again," James said, a smile on his face.

I'd always wondered how I'd share the news of my pregnancy to those I loved. I'd envisioned all the cute and creative ways I could do it, especially after being the recipient of such news from others. When faced with infertility, cancer, and ultimately surrogacy, I worried talking about our journey with too many people would in some way take away the excitement I'd have telling my family. The element of surprise could no longer exist, and therefore, I assumed it wouldn't feel as exciting. I couldn't have been more wrong.

That evening, we took two bottles of apple cider, flowers, and balloons over to Allison and Mike to celebrate the news. Having already spoken with them on the phone after they learned of the results from Melissa, we wanted to further express our excitement in person.

And it didn't stop there. In sharing the news with James' parents, we arrived unannounced on their doorstep with a bottle of champagne hidden behind my back. The door opened, and they both stood at the entrance with looks of concern and confusion on their faces at our sudden presence.

"WE'RE HAVING A BABY," I screamed, lifting the bottle of champagne above my head in excitement. James' mom screamed in relief, her knees buckling beneath her. The screaming continued, hugs ensued, and I was able to have a guilt-free, celebratory glass of champagne on the day we found out we were pregnant.

The celebrations continued. Hugs, laughs, and special moments between those we loved kept us on an emotional high that'd been a long time coming. Allison was retested a week later, and her numbers continued to look good. There was only one thing that could possibly break our spirits, and we did our best to put any fears in the back of our minds and live in the present moment.

On December 14, twelve days after the positive test, while getting ready for my first Christmas party with my new employer, we received a phone call from Melissa.

"Hi Jenny. I'm just wanting to let you know Allison called this morning to tell me about some bleeding she experienced. Although sometimes normal to bleed at the beginning of pregnancy, this sounded like more than we felt comfortable with, so she came in to run a few tests." I felt nauseous and immediately sat on the couch.

"The numbers indicate things are still progressing, but I wanted to let you know what happened. We have her on the schedule to come in tomorrow for an ultrasound to get a better idea of what is going on." Despite the nature of the call, her tone was reassuring and left me feeling confident that everything was going to be okay. Having been on the receiving end of so much devastating and shocking news in the last year, I'd become familiar with tones. If nothing else, I didn't feel the need to borrow trouble or worry about what might come of this development.

The following day, James, Allison, and I went to the clinic for the ultrasound. The thirty-minute car ride was pleasant, but noticeably quiet. We couldn't avoid the reason we were making the drive, but also didn't want to overreact. It felt responsible to reserve our reaction until we knew more.

Once checked in and in the exam room, the on-call doctor came in to meet with us. "Looks like we're here to see what is causing some bleeding?" she asked. A few moments later, we looked at the monitor, hoping we'd see something positive.

"That's your baby right there," she said, pointing at a small, round circle on the screen. "Can you see that flickering? It's faint, but it's there." Relief washed over me hearing her say there was a heartbeat, not to mention being able to see it for myself. That was my baby. Proof of the only DNA I'd ever be capable of passing on to create a life. The pulsing image reminded me of a cursor in a Word document, only smaller and faster. And just as quickly as it appeared on the screen, the image was gone.

The exam discovered a subchorionic hemorrhage, bleeding under one of the membranes surrounding the embryo. Common in early pregnancy, it happens when the placenta partially detaches from the site of implantation on the uterine wall. Nothing notably causes it to happen and bed rest is the only remedy. We were instructed to come back four days later and see Dr. Fry to follow up.

CHAPTER 20

The afternoon of Thursday, December 19, Mike, Allison, and I drove together to the clinic, and James planned to meet us there, having gone into work that morning. Allison followed the orders to stay off her feet and hadn't seen or felt anything to cause further concern over the days between visits.

"I'm so sorry, Dr. Fry was double booked today, so we're going to have one of his nurses come in and do the exam," the receptionist told me when I approached to check in. Feeling confident everything was fine, I didn't push for Dr. Fry to be present.

Our exam room was larger than any we'd recently been in, but much of the space remained empty. The sink was designed to look like the head of a sperm, with a tail painted on the countertop. I wondered what the motility of *that* sperm would be and laughed to myself.

"I'm running late, but I'm on my way. I'll explain what happened when I get there!" James said, frantically answering his phone when I called to see where he was. Having taken Gus to daycare on his way to work, he had to drop him off at home before heading to our appointment.

After waiting roughly fifteen minutes, James rushed through the door, frazzled and out of breath. "Oh my God, I'm sorry!" he said, removing his coat frantically while he spoke. The nurse went to see another patient after I informed her of the delay.

"I picked up Gus, and on the way home it started to smell like shit. Like, bad. I looked in the backseat, and there was diarrhea all over." He went on to describe frantically speeding down the freeway in his Jeep Cherokee, knowing he was already late for our appointment but also wanting to clean the mess as quickly as possible. "Unfortunately, the car still smells like shit," he said. He looked at his hands to ensure he'd washed them thoroughly and made his way to the sink for good measure.

"Is this supposed to be a giant sperm?" he asked, suddenly distracted by the cleverness of the design. All four of us laughed until a small knock on the door, followed by the nurse entering, brought us back to the reality of where we were.

The exam began, and it took only a moment to realize the nurse hadn't been able to locate a heartbeat. It seemed to happen in unison, the entire room suddenly quiet and focused. The nurse twirled the ultrasound wand back and forth, trying to get a clearer image.

"Is something wrong?" I asked, my heart pounding so loudly I thought they would mistake it for the baby's.

"Well," she said, tilting her head to the left. "I'm just not getting the image I'd like to see. I'll keep trying." A few minutes went by, and nothing changed. No image popped up on the screen, no whooshing sound could be heard through the speakers. "I'm going to see if another nurse can come in and get a better look." She removed the wand and placed it back in its holster.

"I'm sorry." She looked me directly in the eyes before leaving the room. Everything in my periphery went fuzzy, and the only thing that seemed to be in focus was her furrowed brow and her perfectly drawn eyeliner. The sympathy she exuded felt as if a physical object hit me directly in the face. We all sat in silence, stealing glances at one another. The only sound breaking our collective silence was "Holly Jolly Christmas" playing over the speakers. *What a stupid song.*

After what felt like an eternity, a second nurse maneuvered the wand in a similar fashion, although seemingly a bit more frantic.

*Come on, dammit. Please...*I exhaled as I begged. *Find my baby.* Another few moments of searching led to the realization our sweet little EmbryLowe's heartbeat was nowhere to be found.

"I'm so sorry, I just can't find the heartbeat," the nurse said, hesitant and apologetic, news I knew she didn't want to deliver. I wanted nothing more in that moment than to trade my heart with that of my sweet baby. I drew in a deep breath, holding the air in my lungs with the hope that somehow, I could magically breathe life into EmbryLowe. The pain grew to be too much, and I exhaled slowly, hoping the heaviness in my chest would lighten. It didn't. I looked over to see James crying. I squeezed Allison's hand, realizing she was softly crying as well. Lying on her back, the tears streaked from her eyes and pooled in her ears. Mike gently stroked her head.

"Is Dr. Fry not able to come in and talk to us?" I asked. I trusted these women knew what they were doing, seeing as they did this every day, but I couldn't and wouldn't accept this news until I heard it come from his mouth. This couldn't be happening. They left the room to see if they could find and pull him away from his other patients for a few moments.

As soon as the door clicked shut behind them, I turned to James, buried my face in his chest, and sobbed quietly. *My baby can't be gone. This isn't fucking fair. Why did this happen? I just saw the heartbeat four days ago.*

James hugged me, and I felt his body shaking in my arms, suffering this devastating loss with me. I didn't want my reaction to upset Allison or cause her to think I placed any blame on her for what happened. I pulled myself away from my embrace with James and wiped my eyes.

"It's okay. It's going to be okay," I said, turning to face Allison. I leaned over and hugged her. Here I was again, trying to offer comfort to someone else when I was the one who wanted to be comforted. However, if I didn't remain strong in the moment, I would turn into a puddle on the floor. "Something had to be wrong with the baby. This isn't anyone's fault."

I couldn't even begin to imagine what she must have been feeling, not only experiencing her first miscarriage, but losing a baby that wasn't hers. There are no words that could possibly provide comfort in a moment as devastating as this. I was riddled with guilt for having put her in this situation in the first place, for causing her the heartache I knew she had to be feeling. Be that as it may, I attempted to remain composed so we could all get through it together. *Is this a sign of my motherly instinct?*

"We are going to see if Dr. Fry can see something different," I said.

"I'm so sorry," Allison softly whispered. I continued to hug her until the nurse came back into the room. Dr. Fry was not able to step away, and our only options were to wait in the clinic for two hours until the end of his day, go home and come back in two hours, or accept what the nurses told us.

"I'll never forgive myself if I don't hear from him we've lost the baby," I said. Again, I couldn't explain why I needed so badly for the news to come directly out of his mouth, but I couldn't shake the deeply rooted need.

Part of me felt angry he couldn't step away from his other patients for a few moments to give me the confirmation I needed and didn't want to wait two hours to receive. I allowed myself to believe, irrationally and bitterly, that none of his other patients could be going through what we were going through, in that moment or over the course of the last year.

Beating cancer and being left with only one chance at a biological child, I would think his patients would understand his tardiness. Of course, I had no way of knowing what anyone else in the clinic was going through, but selfishly, I felt I was the only one dealing with such heartbreak. We decided to drive home and come back in two hours.

James and I left the room to allow Allison and Mike some privacy. We entered a small bathroom directly across the hall from the exam room. The bright light and freshly cleaned surfaces made the space seem hopeful and inviting. However, the heavy steel door slammed loudly behind us, like a jail cell being rolled shut, locking away the hopes of a happy future. James turned the silver deadbolt, and we sobbed in each other's arms for what felt like the hundredth time that year. There was nothing else we could do.

The four of us walked out of the clinic, puffy-eyed and quiet. There were small patches of snow on the ground, but they slowly melted from the warmth of the setting sun in the distance.

Mike and Allison got into their car. I headed toward the Jeep with

James. He opened the door for me, and I sluggishly climbed in. I was hit with the sharp reminder Gus has chosen this day, of all days, to defecate in the back seat, the stench permeating strongly through the air. If my mood could have taken a physical form, it most certainly would've been the smell of shit still lingering in the upholstery.

We decided not to go home, but rather to James' parents' house, as it was closer to the clinic. Between the smell of diarrhea and the anxiety-induced nausea I experienced, I was more than happy to spend less time in the car. We pulled into the driveway and slowly made our way to the front door, knowing the heaviness of the news we were there to share.

We were greeted by James' dad, who was home alone. We sat quietly in their family room, crying, not able to formulate any words to express our grief. A few moments later, the sound of a car door closing let us know James' mom returned home. Sitting on the couch next to James, I squeezed three times.

She walked through the door and frantically scanned the room, the Jeep parked in the driveway tipping her off to our presence. She'd been aware of our appointment that day but hadn't known when it was. She immediately understood what'd happened after seeing our eyes red and puffy from crying.

"No, No, No!" she wailed, catching her balance on the staircase banister in front of her. Regaining her footing, she quickly made her way to the couch and fell to her knees in front of us, pulling both of our heads close to hers. Looking at me, she leaned in and kissed me on the cheek, and I felt her love for me, for James, and for our sweet little EmbryLowe—a love I could only hope one day I'd be able to express as a mother.

Two hours later, another windy and cold drive, the smell of dog shit still lingering, we all arrived back at the clinic. The sun had set, it was darker and felt much cooler than when we left. The parking lot was empty, the clinic having already closed for the night. We knocked on the locked door leading to the half-lit lobby, and the receptionist let us in.

Back in the exam room, it was quiet. The music had been turned off, making it feel eerie. Dr. Fry entered almost immediately; his demeanor noticeably more reserved. There were no jokes or laughing, and I couldn't tell if he'd had a long day of work or knew he'd most likely be confirming what we inevitably already knew. Either way, he quickly began searching and remained quiet. He turned to look at the monitor, but my eyes were glued on him the entire time. I searched his face and body language for any sign he might have different news to share. However, his expression remained unchanged, like a robot void of all emotion.

"I'm so sorry. I know this isn't what you want to hear. I cannot find a heartbeat," he said. "This kind of thing just sometimes happens. There is no one or nothing to blame. And I'm especially sorry because I know this was your last hope." There it was again. Hope.

He had no way of knowing what that word, or idea, meant to me. He couldn't know this baby had been the main source of hope for me through everything I'd battled in the last two years. He had no idea how literal his words were. It'd been my last hope to bring this baby into the world after beating cancer. My strength and resolve eluded me, and I broke into tears, overwhelmed by everything I'd experienced, all the loss and pain.

CHAPTER 21

N o matter how many times I'd been forced to accept I wouldn't be able to be pregnant with my baby, I was now pain-stricken at the harsh and final reality I would also never have a child who shared my DNA—something I'd known was a good possibility, but one I'd hoped would never actualize.

The only thing that seemed to offer me any solace amidst the grief, was knowing the potential of passing on the BRCA 1 mutation was gone. I'd taken every necessary precaution to ensure I'd find any early stages of cancer. It was only through the rather invasive process of IVF I learned the disease was permeating and growing inside my body, silently and undetected. There was something painfully beautiful about the idea that trying to have a child is what saved my life and losing EmbryLowe potentially saved that same child from suffering from cancer someday as well.

The loss was hard on everyone around us. Allison and Mike carried a heaviness they'd never experienced before. We did our best to get through the next few weeks together, including Christmas, only a few days later. The holiday season had a dark cloud over it while we mourned with family and friends.

On December 23, we received a call from James' parents, asking if they could come over to give us a gift. We were out running errands and decided to meet in a parking lot of a local grocery store.

Small raindrops sporadically hit the windshield as we pulled into the parking lot, his parents already parked and waiting. We pulled up and quickly moved from our car to theirs, trying to avoid the now more consistent rainfall. Inside it was warm and inviting as we made ourselves comfortable in the backseat.

"We saw this today and wanted to get it for you," his mom said, handing James a small gift bag and me a card. I knew it was bound to have sentimental value because of the way her sentence trailed off as she tried to hide her emotion.

"Hope" is the thing with feathers
That perches in the soul,
And sings the tune without the words
And never stops at all.

The outside of the card contained the first few lines of a poem written by Emily Dickinson. After reading it out loud, I opened to see there was nothing written on the inside. Instead, James' mom instructed him to open the bag. Gently and with purpose, James pulled out a small white box that held a Christmas ornament inside.

He carefully grasped onto the string and pulled out a clear glass ornament with the phrase "...*and then Hope appeared*" scrolled across the front in gold lettering. Inside the clear bulb was a simple teal feather.

"I know hope has been hard to come by this year, especially with losing EmbryLowe," his mom said. "I like to think of EmbryLowe as a feather that will always be perched in our hearts and souls," she continued. "I thought this ornament could remind you to always remember that feather, even as you hope for what is to come. Because we all could use a little hope right now."

I took the ornament from James' hand, the string causing it to spin repeatedly in circles. It was beautiful. There was so much meaning packed into this tiny sphere. The poem on the card perfectly put into words what hope felt like and how EmbryLowe, now represented as not only just a feather, but a teal feather, would always be nestled inside the hope we all wanted so badly to rebuild.

I knew my heart would ache in a way I'd never experienced before, and I was afraid of being angry and hopeless. However, this gift reminded me even if I allowed myself to stay in the grief and anger, I'd always be able to find hope again, and this trial would be no different. Not to mention it helped me visualize that I could feel grief and hope at the same time.

A few days later, Christmas was upon us. James' parents purchased a beautiful dark brown wooden urn with the intention of holding a small ceremony to honor and say goodbye to EmbryLowe. Because there was no physical evidence of our loss, the pregnancy having been at such an early stage, we decided to fill the box with mementos we'd collected in our short time of excitement—a white stork Christmas ornament that'd been gifted to us, a onesie with the words "the little embryo that could" across the front, our first few ultrasound photos, and handwritten letters to our baby we'd never meet.

The day after Christmas, the four of us convened in James' parents' backyard. The frigid winter air chapped my lips, and the tip of my nose was red and numb from the cold. James' dad took on the task of digging a small hole in the frozen dirt in their garden, hours before. We stood in a circle and read our letters to EmbryLowe out loud. Words were not the only thing spilling from our bodies. Tears fell from each of our eyes, landing on the smooth wooden surface of the box now nestled a foot deep in the ground. I was the last to read my letter.

To my sweet little unborn baby,

I'm not really even certain how I feel right now or what to say. I think I have gone through so many phases of feelings when I have thought of you or have thought of what that loss of you will mean to me. If I'm honest, I was never certain I even wanted you one day. I wasn't sure I wanted a child or that I was even capable of being a good mother.

The excitement I felt, however, when Dad and I were moving forward with IVF was really one of the first times I felt ready and hopeful to someday hold you in my arms. How could I have ever known what would happen next? My dear little unborn baby, it is truly because of you that I am alive and writing this letter today. Had our lives not been ready for you and had we not gone down the path we did to create you, I would likely be the one having dirt poured over me by the ones I love. So, even though I'm supposed to say I gave you life and you should grow up to be thankful to Dad and me for bringing you into this world, the roles are completely reversed, and I will forever be thankful to you for giving ME life and allowing ME to continue living in this world.

The day I found out about you, sweet EmbryLowe, was both the best and worst day of our lives. I knew of your existence only to find, hours later, that you were where my DNA ended. I had so many emotions going through me that day. But one of the strongest was the need to fight like hell so I could someday hold your dear head in my hands.

I wanted to look down and see your big brown eyes and dimples. I wanted to see the color of your hair. I wanted to hear the sounds you would make and hear you laugh for the first time. I wanted to sing lullabies to you and rock you to sleep. I wanted to see what kind of person you would turn into and see this perfect mixture of myself and Dad right before my eyes. I was so beyond thankful that you fought as hard as you did to survive. Of course you were mine!

I mourned the loss of you at the same time as I celebrated and held on to hope. That was really all I could do. I worried like crazy about you, even when you were safely tucked away in Allison's uterus. I loved you so much for the time you were here, and I will never forget the gift you have given me. Life.

I'm so sorry I couldn't protect you. That I couldn't do anything but stand idly by and watch you slip away. I wish I could have done something to repay you for what you did for me. Even for the short time you were here, you continued to save my life.

My sweet little baby, my child. I love you more than any words will ever be able to do justice. I hope someday I'll get to see you. In a dream, in my mind, in a world, or life that is yet to come.

Thank you for saving me, even when I couldn't save you. Mommy loves you forever.

My knees found a spot at the edge of the hole, my palms pressed into the unforgiving dirt, and I leaned in to kiss the top of the urn. The smell of wood filled my nose as I lingered in that spot. I didn't realize how difficult it would be to remove my lips from the surface, feeling not only gravity pulling me but also my emotions creating a stronger pull. More tears fell as I pushed myself away from what felt like my final goodbye. I rose to my feet, after securing a small mound of dirt in my numb hand and tossed it over the box gently. James and his parents followed suit.

After the hole was filled, we placed a flat, yellow-tinted stone, about as big as a legal-sized piece of paper, on top. I set two white roses on the surface that had been engraved to say *EmbryLowe. Hurry home, little one.*

CHAPTER 22

We ended 2019 feeling proud of what we'd been able to overcome as individuals as well as a couple. We looked forward to rebuilding hope that all our pain and devastation would be left behind us. We were certain 2020 couldn't be any worse.

A few weeks into January, though our heartbreak was still fresh, we knew we didn't want to wait too long before moving forward and trying again for a baby. We had several options to consider, all of which would only take more time and patience.

Because we didn't have more viable embryos, we were faced with the decision of whether to continue down the path of surrogacy via egg or embryo donation, or if we should investigate adoption, something we'd not previously considered.

While discussing the various fertility issues openly with many of my old coworkers, I learned of a few who had pursued adoption to grow their family, and it never appeared easy or seamless. I had minimal knowledge and truthfully was intimidated by the process.

I'd also heard, through a few reputable sources, discouraging facts around some of the legal issues involved. It was my understanding in the state of Utah, the birth parents had certain legal rights to the child up to a year after the birth. I admit this may not have been accurate information, but was enough to give me pause and doubt whether adoption was the right path for us.

However, my intimidation of the process was not the sole, or even biggest factor behind my lack of research or confidence in that option. I'd come to feel strongly I didn't want to take away from James the possibility of him having a biological child of his own just because the ability was taken from me. Nothing about the circumstances surrounding my loss was fair, but I'd come to terms with it. What I was unable to come to terms with was unnecessarily forcing James to also lose that ability.

Additionally, having just gone through the necessary steps for surrogacy, everything was fresh in our minds regarding the legal, physical, and financial requirements. We'd have to go through the process of finding an egg donor in order to create new embryos and we'd have to find a new gestational carrier.

Although Allison had been eager and happy to help bring EmbryLowe into the world, she'd also been upfront from the beginning about her hesitation at a second attempt if the first was unsuccessful. It goes without saying we were saddened to know our journey of surrogacy with Allison was at its end. We completely understood how difficult this loss had been for her and couldn't ask her to go through it again, let alone so soon. We'd always be thankful for what she'd done for us and felt a special connection with her.

We'd have to start at the beginning with a legal contract, wait for medical clearance as well as a psychological evaluation of a new GC, and account for the new financial burden we might be faced with. And although surrogacy via anonymous egg or embryo donation seemed the most logical path, it didn't come without an emotional cost to James.

Having been conceived and brought into existence through anonymous sperm donation, I'd assumed James would welcome the idea of egg donation without any questions or dilemma. It came as a surprise to me when that was not the case.

James found out at the age of eight the man he thought was his biological father, whom his mom had divorced four years prior, had no genetic ties to him. She explained they'd sought alternative methods of conceiving him and his sister due to the infertility issues they faced. James was left with years of questions about the other half of his identity.

Through high school and college his only ambition was to see a photo of the anonymous donor, even to visualize where some of his physical features came from. He tried several times to get information from the urology clinic his mom visited, but for obvious reasons, they were never able to provide him with anything more than a limited, handwritten health assessment this man filled out prior to donating his sperm.

When he continued to hit dead ends with the clinic, he expanded his search in other ways. In 2008, he joined the Donor Sibling Registry, a website that was created to assist individuals conceived because of sperm, egg, or embryo donation who were seeking to contact others with whom they shared genetic ties. He also completed a Family Tree DNA test, one of the first and most popular DNA tests available in the early stages of at-home testing. However, none of his attempts led him any closer to finding the answers he sought.

Although disappointed, he never allowed himself to feel as though something, or someone, was missing from his life. His mom had remarried when he was six years old, two years before learning of his sperm donor. He'd grown up with two parents who loved him, as well as a closeknit family. His desire to find the identity of his sperm donor turned into more of a curiosity as he got older.

In early 2018, he decided to give his search one more shot and took an Ancestry DNA test, as at-home testing had become more popular and accurate. He found a few connections that seemed promising, and included a comprehensive and detailed family tree, a tree that DNA evidence placed him on. He followed differing leads from the compiled genealogy, digging through social media and obituaries, as well as marriage announcements and divorces available via public records. On June 6, 2018, after a night out drinking and celebrating my thirty-fourth birthday, he found not only his branch, but his leaf.

"Oh my God, Jen," he said, sitting upright in our bed as I drunkenly tried to fall asleep next to him. "I think I just found him."

"Who did you find?" I asked, slurring my speech, only half awake.

He held his phone out to show me a photo he found on a LinkedIn profile. The image was sobering to see. The man on the screen was the spitting image of James, only with more gray in his hair and beard. I couldn't believe what I saw, almost as if a glance into what future James would look like. Their eyes were the same shape, including the same wrinkles that formed when they smiled.

Not only was the resemblance uncanny, but the LinkedIn profile listed the exact same field of study the donor had filled out on the clinic's health assessment. There was no doubt James had found his sperm donor. Now the question was, did he want to do anything more with this discovery?

He sat with this information for several months, wavering between being satisfied with only a few photos, having seen a few more after I shamelessly searched deeper on Facebook, or if he wanted to reach out and try to make a connection. His biggest concern was he didn't want to uproot or cause any problems in this man's life. He couldn't make any assumptions about how he'd be received or if this man had told his wife and kids, assuming he had both. However, it was mostly delicate because James knew his donor purposefully donated anonymously and may not want to know about or have anything to do with James.

After several months of deep contemplation, James decided he wanted to reach out, with no expectation but to thank this man for his gift of life. James knew he didn't need anything from his donor and would be completely fine if he never heard back but felt strongly he wanted to express his gratitude. The LinkedIn profile James found listed what appeared to be a personal email address.

"I have no idea what to title this email," James said to me in late November 2018, after he'd written and re-written several times the email he wanted to send. "What if he has a secretary or someone else has access to his emails? Or what if he doesn't even use this address?" He finally settled on labeling the email "Personal Matter" and made one of the most intimidating decisions of his life, hitting "send."

A few days later, after constantly checking to see if he'd received a response, a reply finally appeared in his inbox. Short and succinct, his donor acknowledged having received James' email, saying it must have been one of the most profound messages James ever sent. He stated he would reply in more detail later, as he was traveling and not able to wrap his head around everything. He concluded by saying, "Take a few deep breaths. I have found myself doing that several times over the last few days." With that, the door had been knocked on and slightly pulled open on a mystery James had lived with his entire life.

After a few more exchanges over the next several months, including conversations around my cancer diagnosis in early 2019, James and his donor decided it was appropriate and desirable to meet in person. On June 4, 2019, almost one year exactly after James showed me the first picture from LinkedIn, the two of them met in a park in Salt Lake City. Since that day, they stayed in contact, including a few more in-person interactions and introductions to his wife and kids.

The roller coaster of emotions James experienced during his life questioning the unknown half of his identity, coupled with concerns related to my inability to have a biological child, led to James' understandable hesitation to pursue egg donation.

Initially, we considered the idea of using a donated embryo. It would bear no biological tie to either of us, which initially appealed to James, who felt badly he could still share his DNA with a child and I couldn't. However, we learned if we were to use an embryo with no genetic connection to at least one of us, we'd have to go through the legal process of adopting the baby once it was born. Having a baby via surrogacy was already a complicated enough process. The idea of then having to go through an adoption took this option off the table early on.

"I'm worried I won't be able to assuage the guilt I feel," James said one day as we further discussed egg donation. We sat next to each other on our living room couch, our hands intertwined in my lap. "I'm scared I'll look at our baby and see a behavior or trait of mine and want to be happy. Then look over and see you watching me have that moment and feel immensely sad you never get to experience it the same way." He kept his gaze steady with mine and paused. I knew the wheels in his head were spinning, and he was trying to find the best way to express his fears.

"You're the most beautiful person, inside and out. I want so badly for our child to have your characteristics, not only through watching you, but because you passed them on. I feel awful thinking you've lost that."

James was a sensitive soul and always knew how to comfort me and say things I needed to hear to help me heal. I could understand his fear, because, in all honesty, I worried about it as well. I worried our baby would look just like him and I'd be jealous. I worried I wouldn't connect with my child because not only was I still not able to carry it, but now, there'd be no physical resemblance. I worried I'd be having a bad day and a stranger would comment on how cute our baby was and how much he or she looked like me and I'd snap in anger or have an emotional breakdown. I worried someday, in a teenage rage, my child would yell at me that I wasn't their "real" mom, and it would break me to the core.

These fears were real, and they bothered me, but they were going to be there regardless of whether our child shared James' DNA or not. They were things I'd have to face and overcome, and I couldn't put any blame on him for what card I'd been dealt. I most certainly couldn't justify taking away his ability to have a biological child of his own.

I often wondered if I'd connect more with my child if, when I looked at them, I saw a glimpse of James. After all, I'd chosen to spend the rest of my life with him and loved him more than anyone else in the world. How could that not be true for my child if I saw the same bright blue eyes staring back at me?

What mattered the most to me was we'd become parents, our baby would be healthy, and we'd raise our child together. I'd see myself mirrored back in other ways. I'd be a good example and show kindness. I would be supportive and caring, and I'd teach him or her to be genuine and trustworthy. Most of all, I'd exude strength and compassion only to prove no matter what life throws at you, having those attributes will help you get through any trial and come out better for it.

After a few more similar conversations, we ultimately decided to continue our journey through egg donation and surrogacy. I called Melissa to ask if she could provide insights into how to find an egg donor, as this was one more step onto an unknown path we were going to take.

CHAPTER 23

A lthough the fertility clinic didn't have a formal database of women offering to become a surrogate, they did have one for women willing to go through a cycle of IVF to donate their eggs. Nothing was as straightforward as it seemed in the world of infertility, and as we would soon find out this process was no exception.

We were quickly made aware of the additional financial burden egg donation would entail and had a few decisions to make. It was standard for egg donors to receive a flat fee for just being a donor, a cost we knew we couldn't avoid. We then learned we'd be responsible to pay for all the medications and the egg extraction. In turn, we'd have ownership, for lack of a better word, of all the eggs retrieved.

However, there was no way to guarantee the number of eggs we'd receive, as it can be different for every woman and every cycle. For example, we'd spent close to $10,000 in medications and $15,000 in procedural costs for my one cycle of IVF, which only yielded three eggs and, ultimately, one viable embryo. The idea of spending that kind of money, and not being able to utilize insurance through my employer benefit, added a gigantic amount of stress, especially not knowing how many eggs we would end up with.

There was, however, a second option available to help reduce the cost, called a "split cycle." If we could find someone known for being a high egg producer (i.e., she'd been through IVF before and had produced an above-average number of eggs during the cycle), we could split the cost of IVF as well as the compensation for the donor, with a reputable national egg bank. This meant we'd receive half of the eggs retrieved and the donor bank would receive the other half, to eventually be used by other couples in need. Even though the cost would be significantly lower, we knew it meant our child would possibly have genetic ties to a larger number of people and wondered what impact that could have down the road.

"I'm going to send you an email with a link to our database," Melissa said during a phone call. "Once you get in there, you'll be able to narrow your search by setting parameters such as age, height, weight, ethnicity, etc. However, there isn't a way to filter by 'split cycle' eligible donors. So if that's the route you want to take and you find a donor you like, I can let you know if they qualify." Although the split cycle option seemed more appealing, it did mean the pool of candidates would be significantly reduced and wouldn't allow us as much flexibility in our options. I worried I'd find a donor I really wanted, and she wouldn't be eligible for the split cycle.

"You'll also be able to see a few photos of the donor as a child. We don't post their photos as an adult, but I have access to pictures here in the clinic you can look at when you come in."

Moments later, an email appeared in my inbox, and I rushed to open it, highly anxious to see what our options were. It was like the excitement of tearing through wrapping paper on Christmas as a kid. Getting to see what hid behind the images of snowmen and snowflakes couldn't be done fast enough. I clicked the link and followed the prompts to set up an account.

The database housed over three hundred profiles to view, and I started by setting a few simple filters to narrow down my options: brown hair, brown eyes, five feet five inches tall, and Caucasian. I hit the search button and was shocked to see the list in front of me slim down to twelve donors, although a bit relieved it might make our decisions easier than I'd originally thought. Immediately, the thumbnail image of a young girl in a blue dress caught my attention because it reminded me of a similar photo of myself as a child. I clicked on her profile first.

I read through her medical and family history, her self-rated proficiencies in music, math, and science and scrolled through a few other photos she'd posted. The photos appeared to be elementary school pictures and revealed an olive complexion, big brown eyes, and thick brown hair. I marked her as a "favorite" and moved on to the next profile. I didn't allow myself to get too attached to any one donor, seeing as I wouldn't know if they qualified for the split cycle until we met with Melissa.

A few days later, on a cold, dark evening at the end of January, James and I were once again welcomed into Melissa's office. Having not seen her since April of the previous year, when I was still going through treatment and completely bald, she did a double take upon seeing me, my hair having grown out enough to barely cover my head.

"You know, I'd forgotten what you looked like," she said after a few moments of small talk. "Right when I saw you, one of our donors, who happens to be a high egg producer, popped into my head. I think you two look a lot alike, let me show you." She scrolled through the hundreds of profiles housed on the office iPad she held and stopped when she found the one she'd been looking for.

"As I said on the phone, we have the pictures of the donors as adults here in the office, but we don't put them in the online database for privacy reasons." She must've known people would screenshot the pictures published online, much like I'd done.

When she handed me the iPad, I looked to see a beautiful woman with long brown hair, brown eyes hiding behind glasses, and a dimple in the same spot as me when I smiled. The photo showed her standing on a bridge in Venice with her husband, much like an image of James and me on our honeymoon.

We continued to scroll, as if perusing a Tinder profile, and saw more images of her hiking or posing with her newly acquired bachelor's degree. And then, on the last swipe of my finger to the left, the photo of a young girl wearing a blue dress came into view.

"Holy shit!" I exclaimed, not even trying to hide my surprise. "This is the same profile I saw the other day online and marked as a favorite." I turned to James, making sure he could see the picture clearly. We hadn't had time before meeting with Melissa to look at the online database together.

"I saw this one, too," he said. "It made me think of that one of you in a similar blue dress." The fact Melissa thought of this donor, free of any bias or knowledge I'd marked her as my only "favorite," made goosebumps appear up and down my arms and legs.

Not being believers in fate, there was something about how this happened, coupled with the fact we could do a split cycle and pay half the cost, made both of us immediately agree this was the person whose DNA we'd use to have our baby. A strange feeling of comfort and relief washed over me. This had been so much easier than I'd expected, and it gave me hope our time to become parents was getting closer.

I didn't look at her and feel jealousy, but somehow saw a piece of myself. It was bizarre to see so many similarities even though we were complete strangers. I was drawn to her, and the fear I'd had of not seeing myself reflected when I looked at my child washed away. I became excited to see what our baby would look like.

By the end of that week, our donor was ready, a new IVF schedule was made, and we had a freshly printed cashier's check in hand to cover all the associated costs. We signed a few documents giving us all legal rights to any eggs retrieved fourteen days later and were one step closer on our journey.

In the first week of February, James went into the clinic to give a fresh semen sample while our donor underwent her retrieval. That evening, we received a call from Melissa. They'd been successful in getting a total of thirty-eight eggs, of which nineteen were immediately fertilized with James' sperm. The other nineteen were sent out of state to the egg donor bank. Five days later, we learned nine embryos had successfully matured and been frozen.

Prior to being put on ice, cells from each embryo were collected and sent to a genetics lab in California to be tested for any kind of chromosomal abnormalities. We'd skipped this step with EmbryLowe due to our desire, at the time, of completing a fresh cycle. Testing required embryos to be frozen, and results could take weeks to get back, time we originally thought we didn't have.

Roughly fifteen days after being sent to the lab, we were told six of our embryos were viable and healthy. Three of our embryos had shown markers for some form of genetic abnormality and were ultimately discarded, a choice completely out of our hands to make. We were also able to learn the gender of each embryo: one male and five females.

I found myself able to breathe a little easier once I knew the donation and fertilization worked. Not only did we have one more chance to start our family, but we had six. I felt at peace with our decision to use an egg donor, and my heart was once again touched knowing I'd found my path due to the kindness of another person. Although I would never be able to personally thank her, I could only hope my gratitude would be present every day, when the baby she helped me create was born—a beautiful connection to a stranger I'd be lucky to share.

CHAPTER 24

N ot long after we learned the results of the egg donation, we began once
again contemplating how we'd begin looking for a new surrogate. The
task seemed tiring, but I continually reminded myself this could be the last
leg of the race. I'd already made it through what I hoped would be the most
difficult obstacles and was looking down the home stretch. On February 27,
2020, we once again turned to Facebook to ask our army of friends and family for help. This time, James made the plea.

*Hey friends, this is a weird thing to be posting, but I think I'm ready to do
so. Jenny and I have investigated next steps for how we'll grow our family after
the whole, you know, "life crushing sadness," thing.*

*Despite the heartache, we're still so eager to be parents. I can't wait to
see Jenny singing our baby to sleep, or to have a perfect new excuse to break
plans at the last minute. We've chosen to pursue egg donation and will be
hoping for a wonderful announcement sometime later this year. We're hoping someone out there among our friends and family has (or knows someone
with) a passion to help people in our situation through surrogacy. If so, we
would love to talk with you about potentially joining this crazy journey*

with us. Light appetizers will be served. BYOB (Bring your own...baby? Kind of?) Please send me a DM or text if you have any leads.

Thank you, from the bottom of my heart, for all your support and love over the last year, particularly after we lost EmbryLowe. I can't tell you enough how much the comments, acknowledgements (even as silent nods through something as simple as a "like"), and thoughtful conversations have raised me up over the last year. God, the world is still so good. It's been so easy to feel disappointed with how divided we all seem, but moments like what I've experienced recently (from all types of people of many world views) have helped restore my faith and heal my soul. Thank you, thank you. I promise I'll pay it forward.

Now go find me a surrogate, please.

Twenty-nine minutes after making the post, Brianna, a friend of James from high school, responded.

Me!!!!! I'm open to either egg donation or surrogate. I'm not sure if I'll be your best candidate given our history to conceive our twins. But I do have some experience with the process and very much am passionate about helping others grow their families.

I first met Brianna in the spring of 2014. She'd reached out to James asking if he and I would like to play on her adult recreation league kick-ball team. Having not played since I was in elementary school, I was skeptical about whether we should dedicate our time to playing once a week. Despite losing half of our games, we enjoyed the time spent drinking beer and getting ridiculously competitive with other grown adults. So much so that James and I went on to play various sports with friends and strangers we met through the same league, over the course of four-teen more seasons and counting.

In the years following our only season with Brianna, I continued to follow her on social media, but a more substantial friendship never formed. She'd been married and divorced at a young age and had a teenage daughter. I watched as she met and married her current husband, Ben, and saw them face their own fertility struggles. I followed as she eventually went through IVF, which resulted in the birth of twins.

Like me, she'd been open and vocal about her journey, in hopes it could help someone else. She posted about her daily injections, side effects from medications, and the discomforts of being pregnant with twins. I was overjoyed when I saw her babies arrive safely in September 2018.

When I made my post on social media in 2019, announcing we were starting a cycle of IVF, Brianna reached out to offer support if we needed it. I went back to her Facebook page and looked through old posts she'd made, to prepare myself for what I was about to go through. Her honesty and openness were wonderful when she went through her cycle, but it didn't dawn on me how helpful it was until I was similarly going through the experience myself.

Within a month, rather than announcing I was pregnant, I was telling my friends and loved ones about my cancer diagnosis. Brianna was once again one of the first people to reach out to offer her support. She put together a bag of items I might need while going through chemo and left it on my porch one afternoon. It included a blanket, comfy socks, mints, a notepad, colored pencils, and a knitted beanie to keep my bald head warm. She'd been a huge supporter of mine even though we weren't close. When I saw her comment, I was humbled, thankful, and even curious to know if she'd be a viable candidate. And for some reason, I wasn't surprised she would offer to help us. Brianna had always been open about her journey to growing her family and I could see how selfless she was, even for how little we'd interacted in person. *Could finding another* surrogate be this easy?

"Did you see Brianna's comment?" James asked. The excitement on his face was something I'd not seen as profoundly since we'd lost EmbryLowe.

"Yeah, is she serious?"

"I guess there's one way to find out!" he said.

Hey friend! Thank you so much for your comment on my post. I was so grateful for your enthusiasm. Do you think we could talk sometime in the next few days?

Within a few hours, after several messages back and forth, we'd planned the next evening to meet her and Ben over a video call to talk things through.

Although Brianna felt up to the task and desired to be a surrogate, Ben expressed a few reservations and wanted to be able to meet and talk with us before agreeing.

In the meantime, we received one more text from another friend, Danielle, not to be confused with the Danielle who gave me my *Survivor* buff. Ironically, we'd met her through the kickball league Brianna introduced us to.

Hey, I saw your post! I don't know anything about egg donation or surrogacy (since until you told me otherwise, I thought I was too old), but I would do either for you guys! I am so excited to see you guys become parents and would love to do anything I can to help!!

You and Jenny constantly amaze me with your strength and love for each other. I don't know anyone more deserving of parenthood. I am truly blessed to have you guys in my life! Can't wait to see the Lowe family grow! Let me know if there is anything I can do. Love you guys!

Although we'd spent several years getting to know Danielle and watching her become a mother herself, her offer to be our surrogate was generous and unexpected. I was humbled by her eagerness to help James and me start our family. Despite being someone we would've loved to move forward with, her insurance didn't cover the cost of her pregnancy as a surrogate, and we knew the additional medical costs weren't something we could easily afford.

The following day, positioned with a glass of wine and sitting in what had come to be our "big news" spot, Brianna's familiar smile appeared on our screen. Ben, whom we were meeting for the first time, sat next to her. The anticipation of the conversation only built as the image became frozen from an unstable internet connection. After a few moments of their faces being stuck awkwardly mid "hello," the video buffered, and we could see them clearly.

"Hi there!" I said once I was confident the glitch was resolved. "Ben, it is nice to finally meet you, even if not in person!" I raised my glass to cheers.

There was an odd feeling of déjà vu holding this conversation on the same couch we first discussed surrogacy with Mike and Allison. For a flicker of a moment, I felt a lump in my throat and a rush of heat through my entire body as EmbryLowe's grave marker flashed in my mind. The feeling of loss and sadness lasted only a moment, but surprised me, nonetheless.

Because we'd recently gone through this entire process, we knew the important information we wanted to share from the beginning. Seeing as Brianna had already done a cycle of IVF, she was familiar with the physical requirements, and we didn't need to spend much time on the topic. We did, however, want to be open and upfront about the more difficult subjects we'd found ourselves discussing with Mike and Allison, to ensure we started on the same page. We shared some of the terms in our previous contract, hoping that by telling them in the beginning, they'd have time to think about and decide if they agreed with our opinions and desires.

"My biggest concern for myself is whether I will be a good candidate," Brianna said, after agreeing a medical evaluation was the necessary first step. "I've had two miscarriages, which is why we did IVF."

She went on to explain the first miscarriage was caused by a blighted ovum, which is when an early embryo never develops or stops developing, is reabsorbed, and leaves an empty gestational sac. The reason this happens is often unknown but could have something to do with a chromosomal abnormality.

She was able to get pregnant again, but this time, it was an ectopic pregnancy, which occurs outside the uterus and in the fallopian tubes. As a result her tube burst, she lost the baby, and she needed surgery... during which, the doctor found the remnants of her burst tube, as well as the one remaining tube, were full of scarring, which prevented her eggs from being able to make their way into her uterus. This was determined to be the cause of her inability to get pregnant, and ultimately, why she required the assistance of IVF.

"The good news is IVF was successful, and I was able to have our twins. So at least we know the process works!" she said, proudly. After talking through a few more things, the call ended, and the following day, Brianna texted to tell me they were up for the task.

And then, COVID hit.

About a week after this promising conversation, James and I, like so many others, were forced to quarantine in our home, work remotely, and wear uncomfortable face masks while trying to stay six feet away from others in public. At the time, we had no idea how big the pandemic would become or the toll it would take on life as we knew it.

Luckily, the fertility clinic remained open and operating, and Brianna was able to meet with Melissa to complete her medical evaluations by the beginning of April. In the meantime, James and I made ourselves comfortable working from home, our dining room table serving as our shared office space. And we made a new addition to our family, a second dog.

"I think I want to name him Morty," I said, our new corgi puppy asleep in my lap on our car ride home from picking him up.

"Yeah?" James asked, smiling. "Why is that?"

"Well, we already have two other good luck charms from *Rick and Morty*," I said, referencing the Mr. Poopy Butthole pin and the Sperm Rodeo Morty that James gifted me during our IUI attempts. "Why not make it a third?" I asked, holding the puppy in the air.

Afraid he might get scared and pee on me, I lowered him into my arms. "Hi, Morty," I said and kissed him on top of his head. "Yeah, that feels right."

By mid-April, we learned Brianna was medically cleared, although her exam did result in finding several fibroids in her uterus, which could lessen the chance of a successful implantation if left untreated. It was recommended they be surgically removed and tested to ensure it wasn't anything more serious, like cancer.

Brianna knew my doctor had initially thought my cancer was fibroids during my IVF ultrasound. This caused her to not want to take any chances, and she scheduled her surgery soon after. A few days after her procedure, she learned her test results were normal, and we collectively decided we wanted her to be our surrogate.

"I can't tell you how much this means to me and how perfectly this all seems to fit," she responded after I'd asked if she was certain she wanted to do this for us. "I think this was truly meant to be. I watched in awe, as you struggled with fertility and then as you fought cancer. My heart was broken for you and James. I felt so helpless," she continued, her voice cracking as she spoke.

She described how she'd felt during her own journey and how her experience getting pregnant with her twins inspired her to consider becoming a surrogate. She wanted to help another couple facing a similar fate.

"After the twins were born, I was hit hard and rather unexpectedly with postpartum depression. And even if I'd wanted to pursue being a surrogate, there was no way I'd have been able to offer that to you or anyone, even just six months ago," she said. "When I saw your post, I was in such a better place, and I felt it was the universe's way of telling me I was ready, not to mention it was YOU."

I couldn't help but agree something bigger had brought us together.

CHAPTER 25

By the end of April, still not having met Brianna and Ben in person due to COVID restrictions, we'd still been able to get started on the legal contract, and Brianna and Ben completed their psychological evaluation. Their evaluation was successful in answering their questions about how to handle the emotional ups and downs that came with surrogacy. It also addressed fears Brianna expressed about the potential of postpartum depression, knowing it was possible she could likely experience it again after birthing a child that wasn't hers.

The discussions regarding the contract were much like those with Mike and Allison, and we were able to agree on the terms without complication. Brianna and Ben wanted the experience to be as authentic as possible, allowing James and me to be as involved as we could and wanted to be.

"I think it will be important to set appropriate boundaries in the beginning," I said one day while talking about what our involvement would look like. "For example, if you become pregnant, what are your thoughts on how often we see one another? Do you want to keep contact limited to doctors' visits only or are you open to more?"

"For me, the thought of not being able to talk to or feel my baby kick any time I wanted would be difficult," Brianna said. "I want you to reach out whenever you feel like asking how things are going. I don't want you to miss out just because you aren't the one that's pregnant." I appreciated her offer and felt lucky. I knew this wasn't always how surrogacy relationships were.

"I can't tell you what your offer means, and I hope you know you can always tell me if I'm overstepping. Life is hard, and I don't want you to feel uncomfortable telling me 'no.' I just want you to be honest."

"That, I can promise you, I will do," she said. I knew she was telling the truth.

"With that being said, James and I want you to feel comfortable telling us anything you need, no matter what or when. I know this will be our baby, but you're the one going through the stages of pregnancy. Having never experienced it myself, I can't know what you might need unless you tell me." It felt sobering to admit, even though it'd been my reality for over a year, that I was never going to experience what it was like to be pregnant.

Although sometimes glad I wouldn't have mood swings, difficulty sleeping, physical discomforts, or the need to give up wine, there would always be a part of me that felt hollow not to experience growing a life inside me. I could try to play it off to others as much as I wanted, but I knew the deeply rooted sadness this reality would always cause me.

"I understand and will be upfront about what I need. And I appreciate your willingness to make sure I'm comfortable and taken care of." It felt good to define what our relationship would look like and only seemed to bring us closer.

Navigating through surrogacy was more difficult than navigating through infertility and cancer. Knowing there are entire clinics and hospitals dedicated to helping people battle cancer and overcome infertility led to my confidence in the boundless resources available. However, the path of surrogacy was one that seemed less clear. I didn't always feel like I knew which direction to go or what the next step would be. Each relationship and circumstance was unique. Even having been on this path before didn't make it feel familiar or easy. All I could say for certain was trust was paramount.

I needed to trust Brianna would take care of herself and my baby. Similarly, it was necessary she felt confident our home would be happy and safe for the child she was bringing into the world. Together, we needed to trust that those guiding us on our journey were doing their part to ensure everything was done correctly.

It was also apparent this experience would be much different due to the growing presence of COVID. Out of an abundance of caution, our first few discussions with Ben and Brianna were done digitally, as to avoid the potential risk of infecting one another. Having these delicate conversations over a computer screen was less than ideal. As the pandemic continued to gain steam, we knew the in-person interactions we'd hoped to have would be limited.

All the unknown intricacies of surrogacy coupled with how our experience might be altered due to COVID didn't stop us from deciding to move forward.

CHAPTER 26

One decision James and I faced was which embryo we would transfer when the time came. In addition to knowing the gender of our six viable embryos, an embryologist had also determined their quality based on a standardized grading system.

During the five to six-day incubation period of an embryo, the cells divide and develop rapidly. No more than once a day, an embryologist closely monitors those changes under a microscope, looking for patterns of progression, and can assign a two-letter "quality grade" to each embryo.

The quality grade is merely a tool that helps determine which embryo to freeze or transfer. Studies have shown higher graded embryos are more likely to successfully implant or result in a pregnancy. The quality grade does not, however, have any genetic implications, meaning a baby born from a higher-grade embryo won't be any healthier than a baby born from a lower graded embryo.

The first letter indicates the quality of the inner cell mass which becomes the baby, and the second letter is the quality of the trophectoderm, or cells that surround the outside of the embryo that eventually become the placenta. The inner cell mass and trophectoderm are graded on a scale of ABC with A being the best.

Our embryos were graded as follows: #1 female AA, #2 male AA, #3 female AB, #4 female AB, #5 female AA, #6 female BB. For comparison, EmbryLowe was graded a BB, making me feel more certain the loss was due to the quality of the embryo and lower implantation success rate.

When the time came to choose which one we'd transfer, we wanted to use an embryo that would have the best chance of resulting in a pregnancy. However, we became both excited and unsettled knowing three of our embryos were graded "AA," and it just so happened our only male embryo was one of them. It felt like another choice the universe didn't want to make easy for us.

"It's kind of like playing God, isn't it?" James said, one evening while we were discussing the topic. Neither of us took for granted the fact we had six healthy embryos as well as the knowledge and power to choose which one would enter the world. I knew I was fortunate to have multiple options.

With options, however, came an unforeseen amount of guilt. Most couples have no say in the quality or gender of an embryo when pregnancy occurs naturally, and here I was, informed and faced with choices. How was I supposed to choose one embryo over another? By choosing one, the other five would remain frozen with the potential of never being more than a cluster of cells. What would I be depriving the world of by choosing one and not another?

"How are we supposed to ethically make this choice?" he asked, visibly conflicted, rubbing his hand across the week-old stubble growing on his face.

"For some reason, I was kind of hoping we'd only have one 'AA' to make the decision easier," I said, also acknowledging in the back of my mind, I'd hoped it would be the male embryo.

Somewhere along the line, I'd gotten it into my head that I really wanted a boy. It seemed as though fate wanted the same thing, seeing as one of our best quality embryos was the only male we'd ended up with. Because I knew my DNA was nowhere to be found, which led to my irrational fear I wouldn't bond with my child, I'd somehow convinced myself having a boy would be the optimal option. I'd be able to share the "mother-son" bond I'd seen first-hand with different men in my life. There was something appealing about how special that connection could be, and it seemed like the next best thing in place of sharing my DNA.

However, James and I mutually decided it most ethical, not to mention fun, for us to randomly choose which embryo to use. I called the fertility clinic and asked them to randomly assign our male and one of our female "AA" embryos a color. I then asked if they'd email the two colors, keeping the embryo each color was associated with a secret. I received an email back—yellow and white.

On May 15, Brianna needed to start her hormone injections to prepare for the transfer, scheduled tentatively for June 4. We decided to host her and Ben at our house, for a "shot" party. We wanted them to be involved in choosing which embryo we transferred.

When the doorbell rang, I felt a flutter in my stomach knowing this was the first time Brianna and Ben would be in our home. However, my nerves quickly dissipated as we found it comfortable and easy to welcome them into our foyer, not unlike a family member.

"So, I have eight pieces of paper," I said, holding a purple velvet Crown Royal bag I'd found in a drawer. Prior to their arrival, I had cut small squares and placed them in the bag. "Four say 'yellow' and four say 'white.' We thought it'd be fun to each draw one, and whichever has the most will be our baby." Although each scrap of paper was light as a feather, the weight of this decision made it feel like I was holding a bag of rocks.

"Brianna, it seems fitting you go first," James said, taking my arm and guiding it in her direction. She lifted on her tiptoes and was barely able to reach her hand inside. She scrambled the contents for good measure, despite my already shaking the bag before offering it to the group.

"Yellow!" she said excitedly, unfolding the paper she'd selected.

Adjusting my position, I repositioned above Ben's head. He reached in, scrambling the papers for himself.

"White!" he said, rubbing his hands together in suspense.

Next, James reached his hand in. His dark brown wedding ring disappeared and reappeared.

"White!" he exclaimed, more anticipation growing with each new draw.

Three pairs of eyes anxiously watched me shove my hand inside. I was potentially about to make the biggest decision of my life. My right hand shook nervously. I shuffled through the remaining pieces of paper, holding each one for a split second, hoping it would call to me. Finally, my inner voice yelled "*STOP*." Grasping the paper and shaking it loose of stragglers, I pulled it out of the bag, my eyes closed. I filled my lungs with a deep breath and opened the folded paper.

"Yellow! It's a tie!" I said, realizing how serious and intent we'd all been.

"Well, let's go again," James said, wasting no time re-folding his paper and returning it to the pile before guiding my arm once again toward Brianna.

We completed this cycle of each person drawing a color, seven times. Each time, in different combinations, we continued to tie the vote with two yellow and two white. I'd not thought it possible to have the same outcome seven times, but fate certainly wanted to keep us guessing.

"Why don't you and James just try drawing?" Brianna said through a laugh. "Maybe if it's just you two, the outcome will be different."

James drew first but didn't look.

"On the count of three. One... two... three!" Ben said. "Yellow!" James revealed.

"White! How is this happening?" I yelled in a playful frustration. "Eight ties!"

We finally decided to individually write the color we wanted and reveal our choices at the same time. Each of us looked around nervously and covered our papers so no one could cheat. After another three-second countdown, we all turned our papers over. I slammed mine on the granite countertop, much like I would if I'd just been dealt a blackjack in Las Vegas.

"YELLOW!" We all said in unison. We'd all unanimously chosen the same color after eight failed attempts to let fate decide. I jumped up and down, turning to my right to embrace James in excitement. I didn't know which embryo "yellow" was, but I was so excited to be able to find out.

"Cheers to yellow," I said, lifting a shot glass in the air to meet James' and Ben's in celebration. Brianna smiled and held up her water to join in the fun.

In addition to choosing our embryo, Ben and Brianna had come over to celebrate the start of her shots. She suggested I administer the first one, and shortly after, I put on latex gloves and measured the correct dosage.

"There's a target on my butt, inside the circles," Brianna began to explain while holding the syringe and mimicking a stabbing motion. "So, when you poke in, you're going to draw back a little and if there is blood, we re-poke, and if there isn't, we are good to go!"

Although I was familiar with this process, I suddenly became nervous. Not only had I never been the one to administer my own shots during my cycle of IVF, but my hatred of needles returned with force. Heat radiated through my veins, and I began to feel sweaty. I was quickly aware of my inexperience administering any kind of shot and worried I would overcompensate and cause her pain.

"I'm not worried at all. You're going to do great," Brianna reassured me, seeing me tense up. Her trust and confidence calmed me, and within moments, she was slightly bent over our kitchen counter as I came face to face with her ass cheek. I counted down and pushed the needle into her skin.

"Totally fine!" she said, not even flinching at the pain. "You did well! One shot down and like, a hundred more to go!" I put a small Band-Aid over the spot I'd just poked, with James clapping in the background.

By the time we went to bed that evening, I'd already emailed the coordinator at the fertility clinic to let her know we'd chosen the "yellow" embryo. I asked if she'd write it down and send it to me in the mail after we completed the transfer. I wanted to be able to still have a gender reveal, even if only between James and me.

On June 4, one year to the day James had met his sperm donor, Brianna, Ben, James, and I drove together to the clinic. I could feel the excited energy coursing through the car as we laughed with one another. It'd become a joke amongst the four of us Brianna would have never imagined, back in high school when interacting with James, she'd one day carry his baby.

Through the laughter, I remembered the last time we'd made this drive to the clinic was the day we'd lost EmbryLowe. My sadness at the memory, however, was short-lived. This drive felt so different, so much more promising and happier. Then it dawned on me—Ben and Brianna had made this drive several times as well during their fertility journey. We were able to commiserate over what each of our experiences had been like, as well as how serendipitous it was to be doing this together.

Due to the restrictions of COVID, Brianna was only allowed to have one person in the room with her for the transfer. James insisted it be me.

The process was no different from when we transferred EmbryLowe. We spent a few moments in the waiting room, a place that oddly felt like home. Once called back, I waited in the hallway as Brianna undressed and positioned herself on the table.

The soft glow of lights made me feel warm and safe, sitting on a chair next to the table. Dr. Fry, who'd remained our doctor, entered the room, and a familiar feeling came over me. I knew I'd been here before, as had Brianna, and all I could think about was how thankful I was to this woman. I didn't hear any of the words Dr. Fry spoke as I stared at Brianna with gratitude. I'd never felt so certain about anything in my life as I did about her being the person meant to carry my baby.

A few moments later, I watched on a screen as the embryologist pulled the small cell into a syringe under a microscope. She entered the room, passed off the syringe, and Dr. Fry completed the transfer. After Brianna was tilted back to let gravity work its magic, I took my phone out to take a photo of the two of us. I hugged her and placed my hand on her belly.

"Get to work, little yellow," I said, and twenty-five minutes after we'd arrived, we were back in the parking lot with Ben and James, taking more photos to commemorate the occasion.

On our way home, we stopped at McDonald's to get a few orders of fries. Brianna had not only heard it was good luck to eat them after a transfer but did so after her own transfer that resulted in twins. There had to be something to it, not to mention, they were yellow, which must be good luck. Now all we could do was wait. Again.

CHAPTER 27

Brianna had told us that during her transfer with the twins, she'd been unable to wait the full fourteen days before taking a pregnancy test. "I was too anxious and excited to know!" she said."

I'd been much the same during our IUI attempts, taking several tests before the two-week window expired. I knew Brianna would have a difficult time waiting in this situation as well.

On June 9, five days after the transfer, also Brianna's birthday, we called to tell her if she wanted to take a test, we'd be happy for her to do so. Because I knew Brianna and I shared a similar lack of patience, I thought her birthday was a nice excuse to have her take one. Secretly, I was itching on the inside to know if she was pregnant, even though I also knew I was playing with fire.

"Happy Birthday! How are you today?" I asked. James and I sat on the couch trying our best to appear calm while she told us about her day. Prior to our call, she peed in a cup, dipped the test into the urine, and covered it with a towel.

"It's time, are you ready?" she asked, flipping her camera so we could see both the cup and the towel.

"I'm sweating," she said, letting out a long breath. "Okay, if there are two lines, it's positive, here we go." She lifted the towel. The camera brightness adjusted, and the image was out of focus. She picked up the test to pull it closer to the camera. James and I leaned forward, trying to make out what we saw on our monitor in front of us.

"Oh, I don't know if you can see it," she said, the camera shaking in her grip and the image still not in focus. "You guys, there is a second line!"

"TWO LINES?" I said, verifying I'd heard her correctly. I couldn't see a second line, which caused my stomach to sink with disappointment.

"There are two lines!" she said, the smile on her face audible in her tone.

"Stop, where is there a second line?" I asked, my nervousness and trepidation visible on the small screen. James silently watched in anticipation next to me.

"I might have to send you a picture, there are definitely two lines!" she said confidently.

"Yeah, it is impossible to see on the video, but unmistakable in person," Ben said in the background through a relieved laugh. "There's totally a second line."

"Really?" James and I said in unison. Brianna screamed with excitement. "*Really?*" James asked again. I could tell he didn't want to let himself believe this was happening.

"I swear, I swear," she said. "There is a very distinct second line." She was again trying to adjust the camera into focus. She walked outside hoping the bright, afternoon summer sun would provide a better view. James and I remained skeptical and reserved our excitement. I could see nothing more than one bright red line, exactly as I'd seen so many times in the past.

"Try tilting it a little," I said, sounding bossier than I'd intended. "Or try going into the shade, no not that far." I continued to direct her. "Stop right there! Oh my God, I can totally see it! Can you see that?" I turned to James to confirm he'd been able to make out the faint mark.

"I think I'm trying to convince myself I can," he said, his face almost touching the screen. I pointed to where a second, light pink line was clearly visible to me. Once I saw it, nothing could remove it from my sight.

"Let me take a picture and send it to you," Ben said. The text appeared on my phone and the moment I opened it, we both saw the line we'd struggled to see over video, clear as day.

"YOU GUYS ARE HAVING A BABY!" Brianna shouted. James and I screamed in unison, and both started to cry. I let my fear and anxiety be washed away as a wave of relief crashed into my body and left me feeling like I was gasping for air. I was finally going to be a mother.

The following day, I walked to our mailbox and pulled out a letter from the fertility clinic. I knew it had to be information I'd asked them to send revealing the gender of our now implanted embryo. I held it to the light to see if I could make out anything written on the page securely sealed inside. Nothing.

I went into the house and greeted James at his now placed on our ground level, after we both moved from the kitchen table to our own separate spaces. Working from home seemed a temporary necessity during a global pandemic, but when it turned out to be more long-term, we decided to find our own corners of the house for work.

"Look what came today," I said, waving the envelope in the air like Charlie Bucket when finding the last golden ticket in *Willy Wonka and the Chocolate Factory*. I didn't want to let the envelope out of my grip.

"I think we should just open it," I said, "I mean, we already know she's pregnant, what are we waiting for?"

James had always been a much more patient person than me and probably would have been able to wait until the day our baby was born to find out what we were having. With a little bit of persistence, I was able to get him to agree to open the letter. However, we both still wanted it to be done in a more exciting fashion than just ripping open the envelope and reading it together. As I contemplated how we would reveal the gender, I couldn't help but feel a bit of anxiety.

Because we didn't complete genetic testing on EmbryLowe we'd never learned the gender. Although I'd wonder for the rest of my life if my DNA created a boy or a girl, I was somewhat glad we hadn't been able to give it that level of identity. I was certain the loss would have been much harder to come to terms with if we'd known that information.

Although I was scared we were getting ahead of ourselves too quickly, I was also eager to have something exciting to hold on to. I hoped it would make everything feel more real and somehow more sustainable. With that, I turned once again to Brianna for help.

Later that evening, James and I arrived at Ben and Brianna's house. I'd picked up supplies for our reveal earlier in the day and dropped them, as well as the letter from the clinic, on their porch to prepare everything prior to our arrival.

I'd gone to a local party supply store and purchased two large bags each containing one hundred shiny pink and blue gumballs. After Ben and Brianna learned whether we were having a boy or girl they'd pick a random number of gumballs in the gender color and put them in a black bag. Then they'd take the same number of the other color, minus one, and mix them together.

James and I would take turns pulling out one gumball at a time. He'd keep track of the blue gumballs and I'd keep track of the pink. When we emptied the bag, we'd tally our results and whichever color had one more gumball, would be the gender of our baby.

Being the first time we'd seen Ben and Brianna since the transfer and subsequent positive pregnancy test, our first several minutes upon arriving were filled with hugs, laughter, and celebratory conversation. The excitement was palpable, and it was hard to concentrate on anything anyone said. I could see the black bag on their kitchen table, and it took everything in me to not rush over and start counting immediately.

We made ourselves comfortable at the table, across from Ben and Brianna who hadn't stopped smiling. There were pads of paper in front of us both to keep tally, as well as two bowls to discard and separate the gumballs. The anticipation was killing me, even though I assumed it would take more than a few minutes to count and tally the results.

I pulled out the first gumball and placed it into the bowl in front of me: pink. I marked one tally on my pad of paper as James pulled out his first gumball: blue. He drew a tally on his pad. I drew out a second, this time blue, and placed it in his bowl. He marked his pad with a second tick.

The first few rounds were hectic and stressful. We had to concentrate on each gumball coming out of the bag, so we didn't miscount. If I put one in James' pile, I had to be sure he marked it. If he put one in my bowl, he had to ensure I paid attention to counting.

After a few moments, we found ourselves in a rhythm and moved at a steady pace. The sound of the gumballs clinking together as they were being dropped into the bowls in front of us, filled the room. With each gumball I felt my excitement grow. Knowing this moment was one we'd waited so long for, I took a breath and slowed myself from so quickly reaching into the bag and pulling out the next gumball. I wanted to savor the moment, seeing we'd only learned we were pregnant the day before. We'd been in this position before, but it didn't mean I wanted to move past it so quickly. With each tally of another pink or blue gumball, I knew our lives were moments away from changing forever.

We continued this process for nearly nine minutes before I reached into the bag and realized I was pulling out the last gumball: pink. We looked at one another, laughed nervously and put our heads down to begin tallying the number of lines drawn on each of our papers. Again, we both covered our papers to prevent the other from cheating. We both showed Ben our totals to ensure we'd added correctly, and once he confirmed, James placed his hand on his chest.

"James is going to pass out!" Brianna said, giggling in suspense. "On the count of three, we both say our number at the same time,"

I said, not wanting to wait a moment longer. I counted to three.

"72!" I said, turning my tallied paper over.

"71!" James said, turning over his paper.

"It's a *GIRL*!" We said at the same time. It'd taken us both a moment to realize I'd said the higher number. James stood immediately, the biggest smile on his face I'd ever seen and pulled me out of my seat to join him. Brianna screamed again in the background while James and I embraced. I thought my heart would leap right out of my body and do a celebratory dance right there on the table.

I felt so relieved and happy. I wasn't at all disappointed to not be a boy mom. I was going to have a daughter, and I couldn't have been more excited. James would have a little girl that would wrap him around her finger. It was a beautiful start to a new chapter we were just beginning.

And in that moment, as if whispered from deep within my soul, where it had perched, there was no doubt in my mind what we were going to name her.

Hope.

CHAPTER 28

On June 22, 2020, Brianna went into the fertility clinic for a blood draw to confirm she was pregnant. She took several more home pregnancy tests over the course of the eighteen days since transfer and continued to see a positive result.

In fact, Brianna later admitted that she'd taken a pregnancy test two days after the transfer and saw a positive result. This meant, on her birthday, when I thought we were doing her the favor of easing the nerves and anxiety of waiting, she already knew she was pregnant. Instead of being upset she'd done this, I felt even more connected to her, knowing she'd gone against the clinic's advice to avoid taking at-home pregnancy tests too early—something I feel certain I would've wanted to do myself if I'd been in her same shoes. We were so similar.

A week after her blood test, Brianna called me with some alarming news.

"I don't want it to concern you, but I wanted to let you know I've been bleeding a little bit since last night," she said. Her tone was calm, but it didn't stop the dread from rushing through my chest. "I called the doctor, and they said it's most likely a subchorionic hemorrhage, which is common in the early stages of pregnancy and even more common with IVF."

"Oh no, are you okay? That is the same thing that happened with Allison when we lost EmbryLowe," I said, my voice shaking as I tried not to let panic set in.

"I remember you telling me, and that's why I wanted to let you know right away. I told the doctor what I was experiencing, and she told me to keep my feet up and drink lots of water." The fear of going through another devastation caused my breathing to become labored.

"They said if it gets worse, to go in and see them. And just so you know, this exact same thing happened with my twins, and it lasted nearly half of my pregnancy, so I'm confident it's going to be okay." I felt reassured she'd experienced this before without ensuing complications. Over the next few days, leading to a previously scheduled appointment, her bleeding turned to light spotting.

On July 6, James, Brianna, and I met at the clinic for our first ultrasound. We'd been given approval during the peak of COVID for both James and me to be at the appointments with Brianna. As cases continued to rise, many clinics only allowed the patient to attend. Also, we were at a point that had surpassed our pregnancy with EmbryLowe. Although we'd seen and heard the heartbeat with EmbryLowe, we were going to this appointment because it was scheduled, not because something had gone wrong.

While Brianna was getting herself ready in the exam room, James and I waited in the lobby to be called back. A country Pandora station played behind the reception desk, but otherwise the room was quiet. Taking in my surroundings, my eyes were immediately drawn to a little wooden sign sitting atop a side table next to where James sat.

"Hope" was hollowed out of the center of the wood. I felt like the universe was finally telling me what I wanted to hear, and that was, not only did I need to hold on to hope, but soon, I'd literally be holding Hope. Moments later, we joined Brianna and waited to be seen.

The doctor entered the room and immediately walked over and shook Brianna's hand, introducing herself. She looked over at James and me sitting next to the table and greeted us with a small nod. I'd been warned during our psychological exam I might not always be immediately recognized or treated as the mother of the child my surrogate was carrying. However, I'd not experienced it until this moment.

At one point in the conversation, she even referred to Hope as "your baby" when asking Brianna a question. It took everything in my power not to stop and remind her that just because I wasn't carrying, didn't mean she wasn't *my* baby. My anger quickly dissipated as she guided the ultrasound wand to begin looking for Hope.

James and I held hands nervously as we watched the monitor. There was nothing more in the world we wanted than to see our baby, know she was healthy, and hear her little heart beating. We'd been in this same position before, searching for an image showing signs of life.

On the outside, I appeared calm and collected, but on the inside, my stomach churned with nerves. I was scared we wouldn't be able to see her because it was still too early, or Brianna's bleeding had been worse than we thought. However, there was no mistaking the gummy-bear-looking baby that appeared on the screen immediately.

"There is the gestational sac, do you see that big black circle?" the doctor asked, pointing to the spot on her monitor. *Thank God. There's my baby.* My breath escaped me. A moment later, the silence in the quiet room was filled with the sound of our miracle. *Woosha, woosha, woosha, wooshsa, woosha.*

Hearing your baby's heart beating for the first time is nothing short of magical. Knowing what it took to arrive at that moment made it even more special. James and I locked eyes, our faces covered by N95 masks, and leaned into one another with relief and excitement. James closed his eyes for the last few moments the sound could be heard, as if turning off one of his senses would amplify the sound throughout his body.

"One hundred fifty-two beats per minute, which is perfect," the doctor said. She continued to take measurements while giving us updates on the images she saw.

"I know you were experiencing some bleeding, and I can see that right here." She used the mouse to click on a dark spot right next to the gestational sac. "It looks like it's really small and will likely resolve itself over time," she said, assuring us it was nothing to be concerned about.

I felt relief wash over me, and even as she continued to talk, James and I stared at the monitor in awe. We watched Hope wiggle her little tadpole arms and legs. Even though I wore a bulky, uncomfortable mask, I smiled from ear to ear.

Later that evening, James and I sat in bed holding the ultrasound pictures we'd been sent home with—still on cloud nine and in love.

"Have you thought about a middle name yet?" I turned and asked James.

"I have a few ideas," he said. "But nothing I'm completely set on. Have you thought about it?"

"Well, I guess it could be Ann, like mine." My mom had given me her middle name, and I wondered if I should keep the trend going with Hope. "It just seems too simple. Since she doesn't have any of my genes, I'd kind of hoped her middle name could be something meaningful I passed down."

"What about Jean?" he said after a moment of silence. "I mean, your grandpa's name is Gene, and he adores you. It could be a tribute to him."

I only had one grandparent still living, my ninety-six-year-old grandfather, Eugene. He'd moved in with my parents shortly after my grandma passed away in 2010. We became close over the last several years, and he was extremely excited to meet Hope. It'd been over ten years since there was a new great-grandchild, and he called me multiple times a week to see how the pregnancy was going. It was sweet to see him fall in love with Hope before she was even born, and he often said how sad he was knowing he wouldn't be around to see her grow up.

I fell asleep knowing Hope Jean Lowe was set to arrive on February 21, 2021.

It felt beautiful and poetic her middle name was the only "gene" I was able to give her.

CHAPTER 29

One week after seeing and hearing Hope for the first time, we were back in the office looking at more images of her progress. There was no doubt she was growing and getting bigger every day. On July 21, we officially "graduated" from the fertility clinic and could start seeing our own OBGYN...clearance we'd waited three years to receive.

As we got ready to leave our appointment, Brianna asked if I'd heard of the "fertility tree." As part of graduation from the fertility clinic, we would have the opportunity to write a message on this tree, as a symbol of our success in getting pregnant.

In the back of the clinic, taking up an entire wall, were branches and a trunk, made of flat copper pieces affixed to the surface. Notes of encouragement and signatures of former patients covered the branches with metallic Sharpie. In fact, there had been so many signatures over the years that more branches needed to be added to allow for more empty space to fill in.

Seeing it for the first time was beautiful and heartbreaking. Knowing so many other people struggled with fertility was humbling. When we began our journey, I'd felt alone and ashamed of my body for not doing what it was supposed to. It took me exposing my imperfection to realize others around me endured the same challenges.

Brianna walked up to a tree branch appearing to have been filled long before and pointed to her and Ben's message. I felt once again connected to her in a way I'd not expected to feel. Using a teal marker, I wrote the only message I could think of: *Always keep Hope!*

Amidst finding out we were expecting a baby and the continuing growth of a global pandemic, I proposed the idea to James that it was the right time to consider moving into a new home that would offer room for our growing family. We'd built and lived in our current home for three years and anticipated things in the housing market were about to take a big turn. I just couldn't have anticipated how big it would be.

"I just don't know if the timing right now is best to make such a huge change," James said when I first mentioned the idea. "I feel like that would be taking on a lot!"

Although I agreed with him, there was something about the idea of leaving our house to get a fresh start with Hope that strongly appealed to me. We'd gone through a lot of life-changing moments in our home between fertility treatments and beating cancer. I was ready to leave those hard times behind. Not only that, I also didn't want to set up a nursery for her, only to have to reestablish one later if we decided to move soon after she was born.

We found a community not too far from where we currently lived, as well as closer to family and friends, where new homes were being built. In mid-July, only a few days after walking through some of the models, we were in our realtor's office signing the contract on a new house that would be ready to move into by mid-November.

Meanwhile, we decided Brianna was going to use Dr. Barney as her OBGYN. Although I'd only met him once, I was impressed by how attentive he'd been to the details of my history, and I had no doubt Brianna would be in the best hands possible.

On August 6, one month after hearing Hope's heartbeat for the first time, James, Brianna, and I sat in Dr. Barney's office. James sat on the couch to the side of his desk, and Brianna and I sat in two chairs directly across from him. It was a surreal feeling being back in his office, just over two years since my last visit.

Nothing had drastically changed in his surroundings. The same accolades decorated the walls, photos of his children were still displayed for everyone to see, and the same books lined the bookcase, maybe not having been opened between then and now. To him, it was part of his day-to-day routine to sit with patients and discuss the history and future of their pregnancy goals. But I had changed in more ways than I could have ever expected when sitting in this same seat in 2018.

As I expected, Dr. Barney was nothing but inquisitive, knowledgeable, and excited to help us through our journey. He similarly took time to get to know Brianna and her history, acknowledged James and me as Hope's parents, and was accommodating and empathetic to the sensitive nature of our circumstances.

Having not made it this far in the pregnancy with EmbryLowe, we now faced a few new surrogacy legal requirements. For the birth certificate to list our names as Hope's parents from the moment she was born, we had two options. Either complete a home study, which entailed a social worker completing a comprehensive search and report of our home environment, or we could ask the court to waive the home study by requesting "character statements" from our friends and family. Additionally, James and I would have to write a detailed letter about our respective upbringings, the history of our relationship, specifics on how we planned to parent Hope, and provide photos of safety features we had in place at our home.

The things we continually had to do in order to prove ourselves, no matter how excited and happy we were to be pregnant, kept a continual dark cloud hanging over our experience. There was also no guarantee this pregnancy would go full-term, or that something else wouldn't go wrong.

I wasn't only angry but anxious about taking these more demanding steps, fearing it could all potentially be for naught. I couldn't begin to imagine the additional and unexpected heartache this process could further add, and it scared me. I knew these things were necessary to be completed, but it wasn't without hesitation and a bit of procrastination on my part to finish.

By the end of September, each of our character statement letters were received by our attorney, and we completed a ten-page personal statement. The home study was waived by a judge shortly afterward.

CHAPTER 30

When Brianna was about eight weeks along, James started leaving cute little drawings for me that coincided with the size Hope was measuring according to the What to Expect app. Each week, the app would update her growth, comparing her to a fruit, a movie or TV prop, and something from 1980s or 1990s nostalgia. The first drawing was of a small, blue gummy bear. An accompanying note read:*Happy 8 weeks, Mama Bear! Some Gummy loves you!*

Each week, I began to look forward to what I'd receive next. I never knew which genre he'd choose and was pleasantly surprised at how good of an artist he was. Every Saturday, he'd post a new drawing on the bathroom mirror, on the bedroom door, or on the fridge—always in a place I wouldn't miss. Week nine, she was an olive, week ten a Tootsie Pop, followed by a strawberry, and a lime.

In the middle of August, James and I traveled to San Diego to attend my brother's wedding. Not even being out of town stopped James from making a new drawing for me. I woke up in the morning and walked toward the door, heading to the kitchen for my morning coffee. Taped to the dark brown, wooden door, was a brightly colored yellow lemon. The note read: *You're going to be the best LEMOM ever, Mama! Love you already!* I squealed out loud with excitement. I knew the next few months were going to feel long but looking forward to a new drawing each week helped pass the time.

While out of town, our house was placed on the market, and by the time we returned home, we'd received a few offers. Not long after, we accepted one and were under contract. Unfortunately, we weren't able to rent our space back, and our new home wouldn't be finished by our move-out date. We began looking for Airbnbs to rent for the sixto eight-week window between moves.

I sometimes compared the prospect of our move to being pregnant. Because I couldn't take on the physical toll of carrying a baby, I was going to take the physical toll of preparing a new home for our family to settle. Any time I felt stressed about our living situation, I'd think of Brianna, stressed and uncomfortably sacrificing her body. It felt like an appropriate way to take on some of the physical burden, even if Brianna might disagree.

Not long after going under contract, I had a follow-up visit with my oncologist, Dr. Lane. I continued to see her regularly every three months since my last infusion to complete blood work and a physical exam. It goes without saying, despite feeling healthy each time I went in, there was always concern in the back of my mind my cancer would return no matter what precautions I'd taken to ensure it didn't.

In the exam room, Dr. Lane stood at the computer and pulled up the results of the blood work I'd completed. Once she confirmed everything looked normal, I shared the news we were pregnant with a little baby girl, via surrogate.

"That is so exciting! I can't tell you how happy that makes me," she said, smiling as she reached out and touched my leg. "I'm curious, did you ever talk to my referral, Dr. Rome?" Her excitement of my news shifted to concern as she brought up the subject of my breast health.

The year prior, right as I'd finished chemo, she referred me to a breast surgeon who specialized in mastectomies for BRCA 1 patients. I'd wanted to schedule a time to see her but was also letting my body heal after going through surgery and chemo.

"I think you should go and see her sometime soon," she continued. "BRCA 1 puts you at a seventy-two percent chance of having breast cancer. I'm guessing you don't want to deal with that down the line, especially with a baby on the way." I was aware my risk was higher, and I knew I'd most likely have a double mastectomy someday. I'd assumed I would wait until I was at least forty to do it.

With Hope on the way, Dr. Lane reminded me once I had the surgery, I wouldn't be able to lift anything over ten pounds for at least six weeks. I'd also need extra time if I decided to have reconstruction.

"Do you think there is a time in the first few years of Hope's life you'd be able to take six weeks to recover and not pick up or hold her?" she asked. It was a valid point I hadn't thought of. I didn't want to turn my baby away because I wasn't able to safely pick her up.

"I think right now is probably the best time for you to have this surgery and remove any chance of getting breast cancer." She paused, giving me a motherly look of concern. "Because, once you've *had* breast cancer, a mastectomy is less effective."

Just one more thing I didn't want to hear or add to my already stressful life. However, I knew even with semi-annual mammograms and breast MRIs, I'd always be worried about finding cancer and potentially not being around to watch Hope, the daughter I'd been fighting so hard for, grow up.

I was faced again with a choice. I had to decide if being more confident I'd be alive to enjoy my future was worth the immediate physical pain and loss of another part of my body that helped me identify as a woman. I knew I had the option to have reconstructive surgery, but there was something heavy about being thirty-six and having to say goodbye to all femininity as I knew it. No more ovaries, no more uterus, and no more boobs.

However, with this heavy decision also came a feeling of peace, calm, and control. I'd lost all control when I found out about my cancer. The disease was taking over parts of my body without my say or permission. I wouldn't let that happen again by risking the chance of breast cancer showing up unannounced. I felt empowered to be able to make this decision ahead of being forced to. This was something I'd contemplate and decide for myself, my future, and my dear, sweet Hope. It really was a no-brainer.

CHAPTER 31

On September 29, we packed our last box, loaded it into my car, and said our final goodbye to our first home. Before leaving for the final time, we took a few moments to remember all the memories—parties we'd hosted, fights we had gotten into, battles won, and everything in between.

We stood together in the bathroom where I'd spent a lot of time in the tub on my hardest days. A small teal ribbon, one James pinned to his shirt every day during my treatment, lay in my palm. Using a black marker, I wrote 7/17/2019, the day I'd been deemed cancer-free, across the thin fabric. We found a spot to hide it, a tribute to how far we'd come. Tears fell from both our eyes as we left the room for the last time.

Additionally, one of my favorite spots in our house was a white wooden porch swing I'd put on our back patio earlier that summer. James waited to take it down last so we could sit on it one final time and enjoy the view I'd come to appreciate and love.

Our backyard faced a small community park which had become a popular play and walking area for neighborhood children, human and furry. Whether playing catch, hide and seek, or running in the snow, this area was one of our favorite places to take Gus and Morty as it was accessible directly behind our fenced yard.

Sitting on the swing became part of my routine, often multiple times a day. It was the perfect place to see the sun peaking over the tall mountain range to the east, first thing in the morning when I let the dogs out. I found reprieve in its gentle motion when I needed a break from work in the afternoon. And every night, before going to bed, I swayed quietly and watched the dogs run around with whatever energy they could still muster.

James placed a small table next to the swing with a bottle of champagne, a bouquet of flowers, and a lovely note that, in true James fashion, put into words how wonderful our time in this home had been:

A house without you is empty, my love. Thank you so much for sharing this place with me for the last three years and giving these walls a soul. The greatest blessing of my life is that I get to take "home" with me wherever I go as long as I'm with you. I love you so much.

We clinked our glasses and sat quietly while taking in a scene I knew would soon be out of my life forever—one I would miss, but also knew I needed to leave behind to find a happier, healthier life for myself and my family.

I'd undoubtedly suffered many losses over the last few years. Friendships I thought would withstand any hardship, parts of my body I'd known my entire life, and a beautiful child I would never hold in my arms had become only memories. I recognized how differently I now felt about loss and letting go. I surrendered to accepting even when it isn't easy, sometimes it's necessary. That evening, we spent our first night in the three-bedroom Airbnb that would be our home for the next six weeks.

In between packing and moving, I'd been able to schedule a consultation with Dr. Rome, the breast surgeon I'd been referred to. In our meeting she explained what options I had as well as what surgery would entail. I was somewhat familiar with what to expect, being the third woman in my family to undergo this procedure. I felt like I was yet again joining an exclusive club, and this time, the other members were women I knew and loved.

In addition to removing all my breast tissue, I was given the choice of whether to keep or remove my nipples. Although something I'd previously contemplated, I hadn't made a final decision. Because I'd never had breast cancer, Dr. Rome said future risk would be less than one percent if I kept my nipples. I was also met with the question of whether I wanted to undergo subsequent reconstruction surgery to place silicone implants.

I told myself prior to my consultation, if reconstruction was a safe and practical option, which in my case it was, I would choose to get breast implants. At the end of our first visit, I was on Dr. Rome's schedule to have my double mastectomy, and I had a new referral to a plastic surgeon, Dr. Howard, whom she highly recommended.

A week later, I was in Dr. Howard's clinic to discuss my reconstruction options. Within moments after removing my shirt and bra, he concentrated on the task at hand and already cupped my chest. I turned to James and smirked.

"Jealous?" I mouthed.

"What size bra did you say you wear?" Dr. Howard interrupted, his cold left hand cupping my right boob.

"36 C," I said, confidently. "Who told you that?" he asked.

"Victoria's Secret." I'd recently been measured and purchased several new bras.

"Well, she lied," he said, his hand no longer on my chest but writing notes in my chart. I looked at James and wondered if hearing I was smaller than I thought would be disappointing to him. He smiled and winked at me, reassuring me he was just fine with the size of my boobs. Dr. Howard took a few measurements, followed by his nurse taking some "before" photos. We'd decided on the size and material of my implants, much like I would have decided on a new car or a new couch.

"After Dr. Rome removes your breast tissue, I will insert these expanders," he said, holding what looked like empty silicone implants. "I will place them on top of your pectoral muscle and fill them with a small amount of air during surgery. After two weeks, we will replace the air with saline, slowly adding more over time. This will help stretch your skin to the new size."

He further explained that once my skin stretched to the size I desired, he would stop the weekly injections of saline and let my body heal for a few months. When it came time for my reconstruction, he would remove the expanders and replace them with silicone implants.

The entire process sounded exhausting. More doctors' appointments, more surgeries, and more limiting discomfort. Although I felt prepared to part with my breasts, I hadn't been ready to consider having nothing to take their place. However, I could completely understand why so many women chose that option. It was a lot to put my body through, but I knew there was only a small window of time before Hope was born.

On October 5, at 5:30 a.m., James and I sat in the same waiting area we'd been when our embryologist called to tell us the good news about EmbryLowe. The room was empty, a rerun of a popular sitcom blared loudly on the TV hanging on the wall corner above us. The sky outside was still dark, making me wish even more I was back in the comfort and warmth of the bed I'd left behind.

We were led back to the pre-op room, the usual buzz of the nurse's station quiet due to the early hour. I changed into the familiar hospital gown and socks and made myself comfortable on the bed. When the nurse asked if she could get me anything, I couldn't help but think, I'll have the "Jenny Lowe" special. I'd been there so many times I figured it should be known all I needed was a few warm blankets. The mastectomy went well, and I was sent home after the anesthesia wore off. On the way home, James obliged my request for the Big Mac hamburger I'd suddenly been craving.

I was now the proud owner of two new fluid drains, much like the one dramatically pulled out of my abdomen by Dr. Zempolich in March of 2019. A strong, unmistakable dread burned in my chest seeing the drains hanging from my bandages. I was reminded of the times the tubing would snag on a drawer or door handle, causing it to feel as though my insides were playing a game of tug of war. Now, not only did I have to worry about tracking the fluid output, which was off-putting enough, I had to do it with two drains, instead of one—double the monitoring and double the potential pain.

My physical recovery was much easier than I'd anticipated. Other than a surprising amount of itchiness around the area that had just lost all feeling, I could lift my arms above my head within a twenty-four-hour period. The emotional toll, however, was much more unexpected. It left me in a dark and depressed state, one I'd not been in since my battle with cancer. I didn't want to talk to anyone or tell them how I felt, let alone see those who offered to come visit me. All I wanted was to lay in bed and sleep, feeling like part of my otherwise upbeat personality was taken away during surgery.

A few days later, I was able to take the bandages off and see my body for the first time. The boobs I'd known since they appeared on my young teenage body were now gone. James stood beside me in the small bathroom of our Airbnb and helped me unravel the tightly wrapped bandage. I looked at my reflection, the tightness in my chest lightened with each pass around my body, until finally coming to an end. Two gauze pads were neatly taped over my chest, hiding what remained below. I couldn't feel anything, the skin now completely numb from all the nerve endings being removed. I closed my eyes and asked James to remove the dressings.

Hesitantly and intently, I opened my eyes and was shocked at my reflection. Between the massive scar on my stomach, going completely bald, and losing twenty pounds, my body had gone through numerous changes over the last few years, but this was a sight I was completely unprepared for.

My chest was unrecognizable. The skin appeared as if it'd been vacuumed sealed around what resembled Oscar Mayer bologna packages. The shape was caused by the tissue expanders now residing on top of my pectoral muscle. I had stitches on both sides from armpit to nipple, which I knew would only turn into more scars. My body was beginning to look like a worn-out rag doll torn apart and stitched back together multiple times.

I gasped in disgust at the mangled remains in front of me. My gaze didn't linger before I burst into tears and looked at James in the mirror's reflection. I didn't sense the same disgust from him, rather an empathetic look of understanding. I immediately began rewrapping the bandage around my body, as if covering myself would change the reality of what was underneath. James lovingly and tenderly helped me get dressed and walked with me back into the bedroom. I got comfortable in bed and continued to cry until I fell asleep.

I avoided looking at myself as much as I could over the next week and a half, even during a post-op follow-up visit. During this time, I continued to measure and record the output of fluid in my drains multiple times a day. As the measurements became smaller, my hatred of the drains grew stronger. They uncomfortably tugged at my stitches, were hard to sleep with, and even more difficult to carry around as I went about my daily routine. After eleven days, I was finally able to have them removed and was pleasantly surprised at how painless it was.

About a week later, the time came to start filling the expanders with saline. It was the first time I purposefully looked at my chest since removing my bandages almost two weeks prior, and I still found it difficult to recognize my new body. Dr. Howard reassured me everything was healing nicely and looking as it should.

"First, I need to take out the small amount of air we put in the expander." He pulled out a long, thick needle that looked like the kind used for injecting seasoning into the skin of meat. It was attached to a comically large syringe.

The tissue expander had a small port meant for inflating and deflating without damaging any other part of the silicone shell. The port could not be felt from the outside of the breast and therefore consisted of a magnetic material which enabled Dr. Howard to find it by placing a magnet against my skin. Once he knew he was in the right spot, I watched as the giant needle plunged into my skin and subsequently into the expander. He withdrew the air, and I stared in awe as my chest deflated like a balloon. My chest was completely flat with only a few ripples remaining from the expander itself.

I was immediately thankful for the small amount of air in the expander when I'd looked at myself for the first time in the bathroom. Despite being shocked at my appearance, I was certain seeing my chest in its current state would have sent me over the edge. A wave of guilt radiated through my body. There were likely thousands of women in the world who'd chosen or been required to have a mastectomy without the subsequent reconstruction, my own mother included.

I'd seen women post pictures of their bodies, missing parts and scarred from the trauma, and felt empowered by their strength and courage. After all, it is just a body—an outward appearance that should have no real impact on someone's worth. I'd been so upset about how much my body changed aesthetically to remember this was the same body that continued to give me life, even when death lingered like a dark cloud above me. I was proud of the scar on my stomach and how it reminded me of my fight. Why should these scars be any different?

As I sat on the table, waiting for Dr. Howard to inject the first round of saline into the expander, I felt weak and vain. I wasn't proud I'd just overcome another obstacle on my way to a healthier and happier life. I felt as though I'd let down all those women who blazed the trail ahead of me with grace and confidence—those who shared their loss with the world almost as a badge of honor.

My eyes filled with tears, and I promised myself at that moment to always be kind to my body in the future. After all, it was the only body I would ever have the honor of caring for, and my boobs were such a small part of it, at least, according to Dr. Howard's measurements.

CHAPTER 32

We were still on track to move into our new home the middle of November, and everything continued to go smoothly with Brianna and Hope. She would send daily updates to us about how she felt and if anything new happened. Although mostly happy and positive, I appreciated she felt comfortable and safe enough to tell us about the hard days, too.

I had pregnancy insomnia until 5 a.m., so I am beyond exhausted today! It's not Hope moving or anything, just my body being uncomfortable.

I just threw up for the first time in my pregnancy. Actually, in any of my pregnancies. I feel like I should get a gold star or something!

I feel like a very tired and very pregnant sloth! I've spent the majority of the last two days in bed sleeping or in the bath trying to relieve some of the weight from my hips and back.

She always asked us for help when she needed it, either with her kids, taking her to appointments, or just to have someone come by and visit.

On October 29, after running a few errands, I paid a visit to Brianna, who recently moved into a new home conveniently close to the house we were building. We sat in her living room, my hand on Brianna's belly, when I felt Hope kick for the first time.

I was the type of person who, when sitting and talking with my pregnant friends, insisted on keeping my hand on their bellies. I would rub and talk to the baby while feeling it kick. I loved feeling connected to a growing child, and true or not, I attributed these kicks to the baby hearing my voice and wanting to say hi. However, sitting on the loveseat next to Brianna, I felt a kick that would forever change my life and hold a special place in my heart.

"Was that her?" I could barely control myself from screaming. Brianna smiled so big and nodded in excitement. "Was that her again?"

I couldn't help myself from feeling a small ping of jealousy to never experience what it felt like from the inside. I would never get to differentiate the feeling of a baby kicking my internal organs from those of indigestion or gas pains, which I was familiar with. However, the jealousy quickly vanished as my daughter kicked for a third time. There was no question in my mind this baby was mine, and I would get to experience so many other firsts with her.

Nine days later, on November 7, James and I went to our new house to walk through and see what additions were made since our last visit. Ben and Brianna joined us. We walked through all the rooms and described how we planned to fill the now empty spaces. The smell of fresh paint lingered at every turn and the sound of our voices echoed off the bare walls. Exposed wires hung from holes where lights and appliances were meant to go, and small pieces of blue painters' tape were stuck to areas needing to be touched up.

Even though it was missing all the comforts of our personal touches, I felt at home knowing Hope was there for the first time and would be living there with us in only a few short months. I imagined her taking her first steps on the hardwood floor in our living room, climbing onto our bed when she was scared, sitting at the kitchen island doing homework, or walking down the stairs in a beautiful dress to meet her prom date at the door. I couldn't wait for the wonderful experiences we would make in the years to come.

"This carpet is amazing!" Brianna said as she walked into our master bedroom. We upgraded our carpet pad to a memory foam material after being highly disappointed in the wear and tear of the carpet pad in our old house. She bent down to let her body sink onto the floor and immediately pulled her shirt exposing her belly. James and I sat by her side and took a few moments to talk to Hope and feel for movement.

James picked up his cell phone and searched a moment before "Here Comes the Sun" by the Beatles started playing out of his phone speaker. He held it against Brianna's skin and moved it around, letting Hope hear the music from inside. His free hand rested on the side of Brianna's stomach, when suddenly, Hope kicked.

"Oh my God! I have never felt that before. How wonderful!" he said, smiling softly. He looked at me, and tears welled in his eyes. Overcome with emotion, he put his hand over his face as he cried. I leaned over and touched his arm. This was the first of many memories to be made inside the walls of our new home.

Two weeks later, after days of packing and shuffling around from our Airbnb, I walked into our new living room after the last of the boxes were unloaded. *How did we have this much shit?*

My chest started to get heavy, and my breathing labored as I tried to sort the mess out in my head. The prospect of how much work it was going to be unpacking our much bigger space made me dizzy. I found a box close by and sat on it, without even checking its contents for fragile items. I put my head between my legs and started to cry. Everything I'd been through in the last seven months sent me into a panic—getting pregnant via surrogate, moving out of our first home, temporarily living in a space that wasn't ours, losing another part of my body.

All I wanted was to have everything in its proper place so I could finally feel some relief both physically and emotionally. Not to mention, we still had to set up a nursery for a baby merely weeks away from arriving; a baby I hadn't spent much time preparing for having been so distracted with everything else going on, including my upcoming breast reconstruction surgery six weeks away.

I cried into my hands for a few moments, the movers awkwardly continuing to work around me, when James walked into the room and knelt by my side. He didn't have to ask why I was crying. He stroked my back and leaned his head into mine. "It's going to be okay," he whispered softly, words I'd heard many times in the last two years.

It was a familiar moment, becoming overwhelmed at the thought of everything I needed to accomplish over the next several months. I took a deep breath and reminded myself to focus only on the task at hand, something I'd learned to do while going through chemo. I felt a calmness spread through my body, wiped my eyes, kissed him on the lips, and stood, ready to face the mess in front of me. After all, the boxes weren't going to unpack themselves.

Within a week, we were completely settled, with pictures hung on the walls and all our furniture assembled. We sat on our couch, feet on our coffee table, and a bottle of wine opened and half empty. I rested my head on his shoulder, relaxed and smiling. We were finally home.

CHAPTER 33

James and I spent the first Thanksgiving in our new home, just the two of us. COVID cases continued to rise, and our families were still quarantining to be safe. We finally decided on a theme for Hope's nursery: woodland animals. We'd purchased a crib and changing table and took on the task of putting both together.

I'd seen the depiction of couples assembling baby furniture in enough movies and wondered if we would succumb to the stereotype of fighting over who was reading the instructions correctly, which screwdriver was needed, or which part would end up being installed upside down. Rightfully nervous in the beginning, I was pleasantly surprised at how well we worked together as a team to accomplish the task. Although, I can mostly attribute our success to James being willing to relinquish control and let me guide, or boss, him through the process. With the crib and a few other pieces of furniture in place, as well as woodland animal decals on the wall, there was only one thing missing—Hope.

Additionally, James continued to leave new drawings for me relating to how big Hope was getting, despite the craziness of moving. He'd gotten more creative and artistic each week, including some being interactive. Some of my favorites included:

Holy Guacamole! We Hass only 170 days! If being excited is wrong, I AVOCADON'T wanna be right! I love you, Mama!—drawn with two halves of an avocado, one half was me and one half was James, with a blue-eyed Hope between us as the pit.

Week 28 in a brand-new house? AND you cooked Thanksgiving dinner all by yourself? AND now I'm the size of the ruby slippers from Wizard of Oz? We're definitely not in Kansas anymore, Mama! See you in 86 days! A small corgi wearing ruby slippers lay on its back, sleeping at the end of a yellow brick road leading to Emerald City.

All of a "spudden" it's week 29!! This small fry is the size of Mr./Mrs. Potato Head, ready to love you from her skins to her sweet (pota)toes. Not to scare you into an early funeral, but you get to meet this a-peeling little tot in 79 days! Eye love you, Mama!! Mr. Potato Head, in a black hat, blue shoes, and his iconic mustache alongside Mrs. Potato head in red heels and a white hat, stood next to a small blue-eyed tatar-tot.

Finally, one of the last drawings of the year was when Hope was the size of the iconic raccoon hat from the movie *Moonrise Kingdom*. The hat was atop the head of a cute little raccoon holding a guitar. There was no dialogue, but rather a QR code printed in a thought bubble. I immediately pulled out my phone, turned on my camera, and zoomed in on the code. A YouTube video popped up called "Rocky Raccoon is 30 Weeks!"

The sound of an acoustic guitar playing "Rocky Raccoon" by the Beatles started, with the still image of the raccoon James had drawn on the screen. After the song's opening chords finished, a voice started singing lyrics written about Hope.

There was a fetus the size of Rocky Raccooooon, she wasn't always like that she was a little lime, that one day will turn into a baaabay.

Her momma's gon' like that, he said, "I'm gonna get that girl." One day she'll drive into town, skip the saloon for the emergency room.

And Rocky Raccoon, who once was a prune, will be in the arms of her momma.

It only took me a moment to realize the person singing and playing the guitar was my brother. Unbeknownst to me, James reached out to him and asked for his help in writing and recording a personalized version of the song. Standing in our kitchen, listening to the words, I started to cry, smiling through the entire song.

We celebrated the remainder of the holiday season hunkered down in our house as it would be our last time as just the two of us over Christmas and New Year's. We wanted to enjoy the calm before the storm. I was scheduled to have my reconstruction surgery on January 4, and Hope was due a little over a month later on February 21.

Ringing in 2021 felt different than 2020. We'd gone through so much in 2019 that a new year seemed so hopeful and promising. We could have never guessed our lives would be turned upside down again due to a global pandemic. The year 2020 was difficult in many ways for so many people, however, a wonderful year for James and me. We accomplished so many things and thrived during an otherwise miserable circumstance.

We remained healthy, busy working, and were able to continue our path to becoming parents. There was no way of knowing what 2021 would bring, but we held on to hope it would bring an end to the pandemic, allow us to reconnect with our loved ones, and most importantly welcome into our lives a baby we'd been wishing and waiting for.

CHAPTER 34

On January 4, I was greeted in the pre-op room by Dr. Howard. He used purple ink to mark my chest to navigate where to make incisions. I stood in front of him, gown open in the front, as he drew on the skin I could no longer feel. When he was done, I looked at the body I'd spent the last two months becoming accustomed to and wondered how different it would look and feel when this surgery was finished. Not only would I have a new and improved set of boobs that would ideally make me feel more like myself, but it marked the last surgery in my journey, hopefully ensuring I would be around to be Hope's mother. The surgery went well, and I was sent home later that day.

I'd heard mixed opinions around recovering from a double mastectomy versus recovering from reconstruction surgery. I'd read a mastectomy was easier because once the tissue was gone, you lost sensation in your chest, which made moving around less painful. Dr. Howard indicated the reconstruction would be the easier of the two because I'd already put my body through the hardest trauma. He was wrong.

Over the course of the week following my surgery, you would never have thought I'd been strong enough to have a hysterectomy and go through chemo to beat cancer. I couldn't believe how much pain resulted from a simple task, like sitting in my bed. My upper body ached, and my movements were more limited than I'd expected.

I couldn't raise my arms out in front of me and barely got any sleep, as the smallest shift in position would wake me in intense discomfort. I became mad at myself again for being so vain to believe I needed this surgery to begin with. I felt weak emotionally for not being okay with my body the way it was after my mastectomy, and I felt weak physically for how easily I succumbed to the pain.

At the end of January, I joined Brianna at our thirty-six-week appointment, now meeting Dr. Barney weekly for updates.

"She is looking really great," he said after squirting warm gel on Brianna's belly. An image of Hope appeared on the monitor. "We want to keep her in until at least thirty-nine weeks. Since your due date is a Sunday and I am not at the hospital that day, let's get you on my calendar a few days earlier on February 16. Then I know I will be in delivery."

My heart fluttered, matching the fast pace of Hope's heart beating over the speakers. I was ready to meet her but knowing it was going to be a week earlier than planned sent shivers down my spine. Something about her arriving in February always felt serendipitous. I'd learned of my cancer and EmbryLowe, as well as had my surgery all in February of 2019. I'd often thought how fateful it would be to have my baby born near the anniversary of the day I lost my ability to birth her.

"Hope is coming on February 16!" I said to James over the phone on the ride home. He was elated at the news, though I could sense intimidation in his tone. We were going to be parents a week sooner than planned.

Time started to feel like it was slowing down. I'd thought with moving, having both of my surgeries, and settling into our new home, time would fly by. But somehow, the days felt longer and seemed to pass much slower. As induction got closer, I found myself spending a great deal of time getting all the approvals we needed from the hospital to allow for James and me to be present at the delivery.

From the beginning discussions with Ben and Brianna, they were always adamant they wanted us to be present to experience such a beautiful and special moment. I was thankful they had such strong feelings about finding ways to include us to make it feel as though this was my pregnancy. However, during the year, hospitals all over the country implemented new policies and restrictions in labor and delivery that caused a lot of people, especially those going through surrogacy, to not be present for the birth of their child.

Under normal circumstances, James and I would be able to be in the delivery room with Ben and Brianna from the moment she went into labor or was induced. But, after the first few conversations with the lead nurse of the labor and delivery unit, we were left wondering if we would even be allowed to meet Hope until she was released from the hospital.

"I was told by someone all four of us could get rapid tests the day we go in," Brianna said one day after speaking to the nurse.

"Well, I was told we would have to quarantine for fourteen days leading to the delivery," I said, frustrated about the obvious disconnect.

I was not oblivious enough to think things couldn't change as the circumstances surrounding COVID evolved every day. However, the conflicting information we received caused me a lot of anxiety about whether I would be present when my daughter was born.

At the end of January, after a few additional phone calls and emails were exchanged with the nursing staff, we received written confirmation of the exception we were being granted due to our circumstances and the complicated nature of surrogacy.

Brianna would only be allowed two visitors during her labor and delivery. There was no question in our minds one of them would be Ben. James insisted I be the second person in the room, knowing I would never be able to have the experience for myself. This policy would exclude James from being there, however, the exception would allow him to join us when the time came for Brianna to begin pushing.

"I know I will be able to be there when she is born, but it just sucks," James said to me after hearing the news. "I'm just trying to understand what difference it makes if one more person is in the room during her labor from a COVID perspective. We live together. It's not like I would introduce an additional threat." There was no denying the darkness these limitations put on what should have been an exciting time.

"I understand what you mean, babe," I said, placing my hand on his shoulder. "What matters most though, is we will both get to be in the room when she is born." I knew what he was going through. I could deeply relate to the heartache of having something so meaningful taken away without any choice. The birth of our daughter was not going to look the way we expected or ever imagined it to.

I tried my best to be compassionate toward his disappointment, but I was dealing with my own sadness and fears around what I'd lost. From the moment we learned Brianna was pregnant, and throughout the entirety of her pregnancy, I was increasingly concerned about being able to bond with Hope when she was born. Although this wasn't the first time I'd felt these concerns, having brought them up when James and I first started discussing egg donation, I'd been pushing them to the side, not completely sure how to manage or even accurately describe them. Even during the short-lived time we were expecting EmbryLowe, I never worried because I knew I would be biologically tied to my baby. Hope was entirely different.

I'd never lingered in jealousy toward Brianna for being the one carrying my child as I similarly didn't feel that way toward James, knowing he was the other half of her DNA. I'd been the one to push for his connection to her, hoping my love for him would lead to a familiar love for her. But bonding with a child who was simply handed to me after being born, a stranger to me physically and emotionally, began to carry a heaviness I'd been trying to ignore.

The doubts only grew as I started reading books in preparation for bringing home a new baby. Despite trying to find resources geared toward surrogacy or intended parents, I was unable to find anything helpful, leaving me feeling alone and deeply discouraged. There was endless information and advice on how to recover from giving birth physically and emotionally, how to create a bond through breastfeeding, and how to navigate the effects of postpartum depression.

I couldn't shake the guilt I felt for even questioning if I could love her the way a mother is supposed to love their child. I wondered if it was possible for me to suffer postpartum depression and worried I would be judged by others if I tried to classify my emotional struggles as such. I was angry my situation felt so unrepresented. After all, I hadn't asked to be put into this situation in the first place.

As Hope's arrival got closer with every passing day, I worried how I would feel when she was finally placed in my arms. Would she recognize me as her mother? Would I recognize her as my daughter? Was it possible for me to resent her, knowing she wasn't mine genetically? Would she trust me? Would things feel natural between us? Would I be jealous if other people bonded with her? Would I ever not worry about our connection, even when she was older? All I wanted was for someone to validate my fears and tell me they were normal and justified.

"Is it okay if I constantly worry Hope and I won't bond?" I whispered to James one night in bed, not certain he was awake. Facing away from me, I took the lingering silence as a sign he hadn't heard me. But a moment later, I felt his body shift in the darkness and could feel his breath near my face as he spoke.

"What's going on?" he asked, reaching out to touch my hair.

"I just never stop worrying about it." I pushed my body closer to his, now able to see his open eyes through the small amount of light sneaking through our blinds. "I have come to terms with a lot of things these last few years. I've not had a choice. But I still always worry that she and I won't have a connection. At least not the way I always imagined I would with my daughter." Tears began to sting my eyes, and through the silence, I heard them hitting the pillowcase. "And on top of that, everything I read makes me feel like I can only be a good mom if I give birth to her."

"Jen, I know you are scared. I would probably feel the same way, if I am honest," he paused, his strong arms now tightly wrapped around my torso. "It is okay to feel scared though, I think it proves how much you care. And I can't imagine how you wouldn't share something special with someone you care so much about already. Look at everything you have done to make this situation possible. Hope is going to know how she came into the world and how hard you fought for her." He wiped my face and offered a soft smile. "You don't have to give birth to her to be able to connect with her. Just look at Gus and Morty and how much you love them," he joked. He always accepted and validated the things I feared and was able to make me feel safe to be scared.

"Also, I can tell you from experience, DNA doesn't dictate a relationship. Look at me, for example. I only recently found out where my genetics came from but have never questioned who my dad is." I knew his desire to find his biological roots was important to him for reasons of self-understanding and contemplation, but I could also see and feel the love between a parent who didn't share the same tie. "I have no doubt Hope will love you more than anyone else."

I kissed him on the lips, rolled away from him, and closed my eyes. I felt reassured Hope and I would share something special, and I would love her unconditionally from the moment I saw and held her for the first time. And if someday she desired to find our egg donor or when she learned about how Brianna carried her for nine months, she would always know I was her mom.

And just before I fell asleep, James whispered one last thing he couldn't know would send me on another journey I never expected I would go.

"Fuck all the books. You'll just have to write your own someday."

CHAPTER 35

As January came to an end, it became the norm to check in with Brianna daily, making sure she had everything she needed during the final stretch. She would give us updates on anything new she experienced or felt different from her other pregnancies. James and I were on pins and needles every time we saw her name on our phone screens.

I'd always imagined being the one going into labor and knowing when it was time to grab my hospital bag, rush to the car, and make our way to the hospital. I envisioned my water breaking in the middle of the night, causing me to wake in a panic. However, not being the one to physically experience labor pains, having to wait for a call or text indicating it was time to go, was obviously not how I'd expected things to happen.

"I kind of feel scared to drink," James said one blustery night in early February after I poured him a second glass of wine. "What if we both drink too much? Would we take an Uber to the hospital? Could you imagine?" We laughed at the idea of telling the driver we were in labor, me obviously not pregnant and us both drunk. It was easy to forget that Hope could come at any moment, seeing as she wasn't always physically in our presence.

It felt like a bomb with a secret time, not being able to hear the ticking sound of a clock winding down before the explosion. And even though I stopped myself from texting Brianna incessantly or having her on permanent

FaceTime, I'd learned to let go of the need to be in control of the situation. It surprised me I felt so comfortable letting myself go with the flow.

On the morning of February 2, we received a text from Brianna.

All right, this definitely feels like early labor. I woke up every hour or two last night, and I'm still having contractions. They seem closer together, and they are definitely more intense. I haven't timed them yet this morning. But I'll start now. You may have been right about her birthday. Mother's intuition.

Although I'd made a prediction Hope might be born on February 2, I felt my body tense and my heart rate increase upon reading the words on my screen.

"Holy shit, James," I said, after reading the text out loud. "Is today the day?" We both sat up in bed and looked at one another frantically. I called Brianna and put her on speaker.

"I do feel like these contractions are more intense than I have ever felt, but I think I need to time them for a while to see what happens." She sounded composed as if feeling nothing. "Let's see how things go this morning, and then we can always go to the hospital if need be."

For the next few hours, my phone never left my sight. I checked and rechecked the volume to make sure I would not miss the sound of an incoming text or call. By 1:00 p.m., I was in my car, kissing James goodbye, and on my way to pick Brianna up. Her contractions were about five minutes apart and lasting close to a minute, but she said the intensity was getting stronger with each one.

Being the middle of the day, we weren't faced with the normal congestion of people driving to or from work. The sun was shining, although not offering any reprieve from the cold winter chill in the air. I didn't know what to make of the situation, not wanting to get my hopes up this was the day, but also, not wanting to discount the possibility. I helped Brianna into the hospital, pausing outside the triage door for an especially intense contraction, as they were now coming every four minutes.

After checking in, we were taken to a small, uninspiring room where Brianna was hooked to a few different monitors. I sat patiently at her side, watching the various numbers and lines appearing on the screen in front of me. I could clearly see when she was having a contraction. I held her hand and counted as the intensity rose and fell. She got through them with ease, despite how intense they felt.

After two hours of anxiously watching the screen and waiting for the nurse to come back to check Brianna's cervix, my excitement began to wane. The contractions were still going but had gotten a little farther apart, and Brianna was only dilated to three centimeters. It was becoming more and more clear, with each passing hour, this was a false labor. Even if it turned into an active labor, it would take several more hours to do so.

After sitting in the intake room for a total of five hours, we decided to head home so Brianna could rest and be in the comfort of her own bed. I dropped her off, with her word she would call us at the first sign of any change. Brianna happened to have an appointment already scheduled with Dr. Barney for the following day.

After a night of more contractions and little sleep, she was certain her cervix had dilated further than the three centimeters it had been when leaving the hospital. However, it had not. In fact, Dr. Barney said it was more like two and a half centimeters. Although this put a stark halt to the excitement we had been feeling the day before, Hope was safe, healthy, and had two more weeks to continue to grow. And that is exactly what she did.

CHAPTER 36

On February 16, after two weeks of more contractions, daily texts, and calls, we finally reached the day of induction.

"The hospital just called, and they are ready for me," Brianna said on the other end of the line. It was 8:00 a.m., and I'd been lying awake for two hours, anxiously waiting for my phone to ring. James was still asleep even through my early tossing and turning.

"Babe, it's time," I said, gently squeezing his bare shoulder. It was a phrase I'd not realized how badly I wanted to say. I expected it to sound odd because I was not the one going into labor, but to my surprise, a rush of excitement and joy pulsed through my body. And I wasn't disappointed in James' reaction.

He leapt out of bed, rubbing his hands over his eyes and through his hair, as if just doused with ice-cold water. No sign of sleepiness lingered, even seconds after being abruptly woken. "Oh my God, okay. I wasn't expecting it to be this early," he said. I wrapped my arms around him. I could feel his heart pounding through his chest as I pressed my head against his sternum. *Today is going to be a good day.*

I took a few moments to gather the things I'd packed for the hospital, knowing we would be spending at least one night there with Hope. Alone in the bathroom, brushing my teeth, I looked at myself in the mirror. The person staring back was someone I almost didn't recognize.

My hair changed from dark brown and shoulder-length, to short and gray. A few more wrinkles formed around my eyes and on my forehead. And although I was dressed, I was always aware of the scars hidden under the fabric. Nothing about my physical appearance was comparable to what it had been two years prior, except for my eyes. I locked my focus on the deep brown, almond-shaped eyes staring back through the lenses of my glasses. I recognized this part of myself and started to become emotional. Not from sadness of the physical changes in front of me, but because of who I realized I'd become.

I breathed out a sigh of relief knowing every change I'd made, whether physical or emotional, shaped me into a kinder, more empathetic person than I believed capable. I felt love for myself and was more ready than I ever thought possible to become a mother. And not just a mother in general, but a mother specifically to Hope—to a baby that saved my life and whom I would spend every day protecting. I couldn't wait to meet her, love her, and thank her.

"Let's go have this baby," I said out loud to myself.

I walked into the kitchen, hospital bag in hand, to see one final drawing from James, taped to the pantry door. It was a drawing of me, from a recent family photo we'd taken, holding a blonde-haired, blue-eyed, smiling baby.

It's Tuesday, February 16, 2021, which means I'm the size of your perfect baby on her birthday! We made it, Mama! Today is the first day of our for-ever, and I can't wait to be in your arms. I'm so grateful for all your love and patience. Now, come get me!

James stood next to me as I cried the happiest tears I could ever have cried.

"I am so proud of you, Jen," he said, kissing me on top of my head. "For everything you have been through and everything you have done to make today possible." I kissed his lips, warm and tasting of the coffee he just sipped, followed by three squeezes.

I waved at James, standing in the garage, as I backed out of the drive-way. He would spend a little extra time at home until he made his way to the hospital.

The sky was gray, and large, patchy clouds threatened snowfall. I could see my breath as I made the five-minute drive to Brianna's, the heat finally warming the car just as I pulled up to her house. Beaming in excitement, she and Ben greeted me in the driveway. Ben would meet us at the hospital after dropping their kids off with family. My right hand immediately found a place on Brianna's belly the moment she was buckled in and stayed there until we pulled into the hospital parking stall.

We entered the same triage door we went through two weeks prior. The head nurse awaited our arrival, ready almost instantly to put on the wristbands printed moments before. She led us back to a room, marked with the number 2169.

Having never been in labor and delivery, I took a moment to make a mental note of what made this room feel different. A familiar bed, couch, and bedside tray were situated near the window. A small scale lined with a blue and pink blanket sat atop the counter. I envisioned the nurses working quickly to clean and bundle Hope moments after she was born. A large private bathroom with a full-sized tub was accessible through a second door. This was a room I was more than happy to spend several hours in awaiting Hope's arrival.

Moments after Brianna was connected to all the necessary equipment, Ben arrived, dressed in an army green shirt she'd made for him, the words *"Labor Coach. Talk Birthy to Me"* written across his chest.

I placed my laptop on the hospital tray at the foot of the bed and initiated a Zoom call to James to help him feel included. He arrived at the hospital and was able to find a waiting area where he could sit patiently, with his screen displaying the three of us back at him.

Around 11:00 a.m., about an hour after our arrival, Brianna was given her first dose of Pitocin to help induce labor. All we could do was wait for her body to start reacting to the medication.

Sitting on the couch, watching her be tended to, was a surreal feeling. Part of me felt a bit of PTSD from my week-long stay after my hysterectomy. Memories of all the IV's coming out of my arms, monitors beeping incessantly, and not much else to do but lay helpless in my bed all came flooding into my mind, giving me moments of anxiety. I was slightly relieved not to be in her position, but a small amount of sadness overcame me that I wasn't experiencing what it felt like to be in labor.

I was immediately struck with a thought. I would never experience a contraction or know how it felt for my water to break, but I'd felt unbearable stomach pains and lost control of my bowels, which I could assume felt akin to water gushing out of my vagina. I wouldn't know the relief of receiving an epidural, but I'd been given one prior to my surgery. I wouldn't be asking for ice chips while laboring, but had done so in the ICU, lips chapped and not able to drink any fluids.

Around 2:30 p.m., Dr. Barney came in to break Brianna's water. In both of her other pregnancies, she received an epidural before her water broke, leaving her always wondering what it felt like. This time, she waited to receive an epidural until after she was able to experience it.

I stood at the foot of her bed, watching as Dr. Barney measured her cervix, after which, the nurse handed him what looked like a crochet hook. I'd learned how to crochet in my early twenties and enjoyed it as a relaxing hobby over the years. I'd even made Hope a small fox for her nursery a few months prior. In the countless hours I spent holding a similar-looking hook in my hand, the constant pressure leaving a permanent callus on my right middle finger, I never envisioned it being used as an instrument to break someone's water. I was certain I would never look at crocheting the same again.

"So, it looks like Hope pooped," Dr. Barney said, seeing signs of meconium, also known as a baby's first stool, in her amniotic fluid. "It isn't uncommon for this to happen, but it can cause some issues with her breathing if she aspirates it while in utero. We are going to need to have the Newborn Intensive Care Unit (NICU) nurses come in and examine her when she is born." His tone was calm, which helped ease my nerves.

"Well, she IS my daughter!" I said, laughing. Our lack of bowel control was something we already seemed to have in common.

I'd always assumed when your water broke, a feeling of relief would come with it. However, within minutes of Dr. Barney leaving the room, I watched and did what I could to help Brianna through, as she described, the worst contractions she'd ever felt.

Ben was now standing at the foot of the bed, his hands gently resting on her shins. I was by her side with a cool, wet washcloth, wiping away the beads of sweat forming on her forehead. A fetal monitor wrapped around her exposed belly measured the progress of each contraction on a screen for us to see. Every few minutes, we watched a black line begin to curve upwards, slowly gaining momentum as the contractions became more intense. Brianna's knuckles turned white as she tightly gripped the rails of the bed before the line on the screen reached its peak.

"Remember to breathe," I said, brushing the rag across her skin and breathing out loud in unison with her. On each inhale, Ben pressed his weight slowly against her bent knees to relieve the pain from spreading into her back. As the line on the screen would begin to drop, indicating the contraction was ending, he slowly released his body weight from her legs allowing her to reset and prepare for the next contraction. She began to look exhausted.

"Looks like you are making progress, you're at six centimeters now," the nurse said, rechecking Brianna's cervix thirty minutes after her water was broken.

"When will I be able to get my epidural?" Brianna asked through the pain, blowing past the update about her progress. "These contractions are awful," she moaned.

A few minutes later, the anesthesiologist entered the room and quickly positioned Brianna on her left side. He examined the abnormally long needle as he made his final preparations. I felt a sudden wave of relief flush through my body that I was not the one about to have my spine injected. Despite its off-putting nature, I couldn't look away and found I wanted to watch, having not seen an epidural administered before. However, the anesthesiologist was adamant Ben and I stay in front of Brianna where we would not be able to see what he was doing. He also insisted we end the Zoom call for privacy reasons.

"That is my husband, he is the intended father," I said. I felt unsettled by his harsh tone and knew I wanted to defend James' presence in any way I could. "He isn't recording, he is just watching."

The doctor agreed to let me keep the call active but asked me to turn the camera to face the wall as a precautionary measure. Disappointed and not certain why I couldn't watch, I followed his orders and stood at the head of the bed, holding Brianna's hand.

During the few moments it took for the epidural to be put into place, Brianna gasped in pain, squeezing my hand so tightly it began to go numb.

Trying to hold perfectly still while lying on her side, a contraction began to rise, causing her blood pressure to suddenly drop.

"I feel like I am going to pass out," she said through her mask, looking at me with tears in her eyes. I watched helplessly, all the color draining from her face. The monitors beeped frantically in the background as the anesthesiologist and nurse rolled her slowly onto her back to try to prevent her from fainting. Luckily, the epidural was successfully placed and within a few minutes of returning to her back, her skin's pink hue started to return, and her blood pressure began to normalize.

This wasn't the first time her blood pressure had been an issue during this pregnancy. Every time she went in for a checkup, it was higher than normal. Dr. Barney tested her for gestational diabetes, which she had when pregnant with her twins. Her test results were negative, and her higher-than-normal blood pressure was attributed to other causes and determined not to be of concern.

"You're having another contraction. Can you feel it?" I asked. The black line was rising again, but Brianna didn't move an inch. The epidural took effect quickly, and she was no longer in the excruciating pain that had her gasping in agony only ten minutes prior.

"I feel great now! Just a little pressure," she said, nonchalantly.

I decided to use this newfound comfort as time to go and sit with James in the waiting area. I found him at a small table outside of a surgical clinic a few floors above labor and delivery. It was a quiet space at the end of a hallway, right next to a large floor-to-ceiling window. Snow continued to fall, and the cloud-blanketed sky cast a soft light over the room. We hugged for the first time since I'd left the house, hours before.

I saw Ben and Brianna on the computer screen, the Zoom call still connected. I was saddened to see the limited image he was able to see on his thirteen-inch laptop. Even though he was present through video, I knew there was no way he was able to take in the day's events the same way I'd been able to in person. After our short visit, I planted a soft kiss on his lips and made my way back to Brianna's bedside.

"I am so thankful, and I just want you to be okay and for her to be okay," I said, a few moments after returning to the delivery room, wiping a tear before it could fall off my cheek. "I am terrified to become a mom, but

I know I have good people I can look up to and turn to if things get hard." I paused, glad a contraction was building, giving me an excuse to breathe with her and fight back more tears. "Thank you so much." I smiled, leaned down, attempting to reach over the rail of the bed, and kissed her on the forehead. I turned to Ben, standing right next to me with arms open, and thanked him for all his support as well.

Ten minutes later, around 4:45 p.m., our nurse came in for another cervix check. "Looks like you are at nine centimeters, I think I can call Dr. Barney now."

I turned to the computer and saw James packing all his things in reaction to the update. It was finally time for him to join us, and within five minutes, he pushed open the heavy door, entering the delivery room for the first time. Brianna similarly made a shirt for him to wear for the occasion. The same army green, but a different message scrawled across his chest: "*Promoted to Daddy. Est. 2021.*" James and Ben shared a tender hug and held each other's embrace for a moment. He then made his way to Brianna, hugged her best he could, and leaned over to kiss her belly.

"Are you ready to come out and say hi to us?" he asked in baby talk, cupping his hands to amplify the sound for Hope. "It's almost time. It's almost time to come out."

Around 5:10 p.m., Dr. Barney entered the room, greeting us all with hugs. From that moment on, things moved at a quick pace. There were suddenly several nurses in the room, all hustling to get things ready.

Two NICU nurses prepared the table where Hope would first be checked, another nurse entered information into the computer, and a fourth nurse completely transformed the bed, Brianna sitting upright with her feet now resting in stirrups. The sound of Hope's heart was audible over a loudspeaker. If I'd blinked, I felt I would have missed everything.

I would sit next to Dr. Barney and be the first person to hold Hope. He asked his nurse to help get me into the freshly opened, sterile hospital gown and latex gloves I was required to wear.

"Be sure not to touch anything," he said, as the nurse helped me slide my right hand into the glove. "You can touch your hands together once you have both gloves on, but you want to keep everything sterile."

"Well, if anyone is good at being completely sterile, I would say it is me!" Everyone laughed.

I stood perfectly still until instructed exactly where to go. Dr. Barney sat at the foot of the bed and motioned for me to take a seat in the chair positioned at his right side. I caught myself from instinctively brushing a wisp of hair from my eyes and asked the nurse to help pin it back for me. My heart pounded. I couldn't believe after imagining this moment for so many months with Brianna and for years with James, I was finally here, waiting to meet my baby girl for the first time.

"I can feel the top of her head," Dr. Barney said, using his fingers to measure one last time. "Do you want to feel it?" he asked me, reaching for my hand to guide it toward Brianna's cervix.

"Uhhhhh, sure?" I said, looking at her, scared I was crossing a line I wasn't supposed to.

"Yes! Feel her head!" she shouted without hesitation. Dr. Barney placed my fingers just inside far enough to feel the squishy top of Hope's head. As I pulled my hand away, I could see she had dark brown hair.

"Are we ready to have a baby?" Dr. Barney asked. I looked at James, standing next to me holding Brianna's left leg, her knees now pressing into her chest. He freed one hand and reached over to brush my cheek with his thumb. A tidal wave of emotions pulsed between us. We'd come so far from where we started and overcame so many obstacles to arrive at that moment. Through our masks, we both said, "I love you."

"Seven, eight, nine, ten," Dr. Barney said, his voice booming as he counted through the contraction Brianna was now having. "Good, okay breathe, now again," he said, still riding the wave of the same contraction. With each count from one to ten, Hope's head came closer to the surface and retracted slightly as Brianna paused to catch her breath before pushing a third time. *My God, this woman is a warrior.*

"Okay, we are going to wait here, and have this baby on the next contraction," Dr. Barney said.

"Oh, whoa, okay!" Brianna laughed in shock. I sat nervously waiting for what felt like twenty minutes, seeing Hope's tiny little head remaining in place, only her hair poking out. Dr. Barney, noticing my concern, took my hand and again placed it on the top of Hope's head, twirling her hair in our fingers. *This is wild, I can't believe she is right there. Just pull her out already!* I turned to look at James. The wrinkles that formed at the corner of his eyes revealed he was smiling under his mask.

Two minutes later, at 5:20 p.m., Brianna pushed through her second contraction. Dr. Barney cradled Hope's little head in his hands, twisted her shoulders, and pulled her into this world. He turned toward me and placed this tiny, slimy, miracle baby into my hands while a small, gentle cry released from her mouth for the first time.

Hope had arrived.

CHAPTER 37

The moments immediately following Hope's birth were a blur. James cut the umbilical cord, and she was whisked away by the NICU nurses to check for any complications caused by the meconium. She was healthy, weighed seven pounds, ten ounces, and measured twenty inches long. Her hair was dark brown, her eyes blue, and her skin smooth and full of color. Soft, muffled cries could be heard every few moments as the nurses cleaned her off and wrapped her tiny little body in a blanket. James and I stood in awe, watching our daughter wiggling in front of us for the first time. We held one another, tears streaming down our faces, trying to take in every detail of this beautiful moment.

Brianna insisted we leave her bedside to go be with Hope while Dr. Barney finished all his post-delivery checks. Everything went seamlessly, and we could hear her laughter in the background as she was being examined.

James and I sat together on the couch, the first time we were able to breathe easy and relax, waiting for the nurses to bring Hope to us. After removing my sterile hospital gown, I also removed my shirt, revealing a thin, black sports bra underneath. I sat forward on the couch, my arms outreached, and for the first time, I got to look into my daughter's beautiful, fully open eyes.

"Hi, Hopey. I'm your mom. I am so glad to finally meet you." Tears blurred my vision as I unwrapped and placed her directly on my exposed skin.

I held her there for a few moments, realizing this was the first time she could feel my heart beating. I spread her fingers and watched as they sprung back into a fist, now wrapped around my thumb. Everything about her was perfect.

We spent the next few hours taking turns holding her. She looked so much smaller resting against James' chest, his hands nearly big enough to cover her entire body. He whispered to her how much he loved her. Ben and Brianna each held her, marveling at how small she was. She never cried or made more noise than small little grunts. She took her first bottle instantly, and a few hours later, she pooped.

"Can I change her first diaper?" James asked. We both stood by her bassinet while the nurse gathered diapers and wipes. We moved out of labor and delivery and were now in Brianna's overnight recovery room. Ben had gone home for the evening, and we wanted to keep her company before going into our own room with Hope.

"Of course you can!" I said, happy he wanted to be the one to do it. I'd never seen newborn poop but knew it would be black and much looser than regular poop. He followed the nurse's instructions and gently began to clean her, gagging a few times at the sight.

"Oh man, I wasn't expecting that!" he said, using his hand to wipe an itch on his nose.

"You have a little shit on your hand," I said, pointing at a streak of black goo on his left knuckle.

"She really IS your baby, Jenny!" Brianna said, laughing loudly. She knew about the time James helped clean my mess in this same hospital. This was not the first time he'd been pooped on by a female he loved. I couldn't have been prouder.

That evening, James and I spent most of the night staring at and holding Hope. We couldn't get enough. The excitement and adrenaline of the day left us wide awake, and we watched her fall in and out of sleep. There were moments we felt scared, with no idea what we were doing, but the fear disappeared the moment she was back in our arms, looking at us through bleary, sleepy eyes.

Before we knew it, after all her tests and vitals were cleared by the doctors the following day, James was pulling the car around to the front entrance of the hospital. Buckling her into her car seat felt like our final rite of passage.

Hope was finally ready to come home with us.

"What just happened?" James asked, lying in bed that night, his long legs intertwined with mine. Hope slept in a bassinet next to our bed, her quiet yet rapid breathing the only other sound in the room.

"We had a fucking baby," I whispered, "No turning back now." We both laughed and turned as quietly as we could to face each other. Our dream of being parents was now a reality, lying next to us. We both sacrificed so much of ourselves to make it all possible. Although I was relieved she was finally here, this was only the first night of many more to come, worrying about every little thing she did.

The first few nights at home were admittedly difficult. We were not only trying to adjust to having a helpless newborn in our presence, learning what she liked and didn't like, but she was also adjusting to life outside the womb, getting to know our sounds, smells, and touch.

James and I worked well as a team, both taking late night and early morning shifts to change and feed her, one perk of not being able to breast-feed. I was so happy to have such a compassionate, helpful partner. I watched as he changed from my husband to also being Hope's dad, something I'd wanted to see for years. We did our best to keep our communication open and honest with each other even through moments of the deepest fatigue either of us had ever experienced.

I saw myself shift from needing to be in control of every situation, thinking I knew the best way to make her stop crying or the best way to rock her to sleep. I allowed myself to equally let James learn how to be a good parent in his own ways. I welcomed help from others when they offered, knowing doing so had been instrumental to my recovery from surgery and chemo.

Hope helped me change into a better wife, friend, and mother. I'd learned so much about myself, my marriage, my body, my resolve, and what I could accomplish when I dedicated myself. I felt deeper sadness and pain than I could ever have imagined while also feeling more support and love than I'd ever experienced. I felt abandoned by people I thought would always be in my corner while simultaneously building relationships with people who showed up in surprising ways.

I learned more about eggs and sperm and embryos than I ever thought I would need to know. I navigated through the intricacies of surrogacy and egg donation, with limited resources or guidance. I was humbled by the selflessness and devotion of others and felt inspired to always follow their example of kindness. I'd found peace and felt empowered by sharing our journey with others. I faced the fears that came along with being a new parent and finally realized love isn't conditional on DNA, but rather, what you are willing to sacrifice for someone else.

Cancer and COVID may have robbed me of many things, but my journey to becoming a mother reminded me how important and powerful having hope could be.

When Hope was just over a month old, she became sick with her first cold. Watching a new baby cough, sneeze, and struggle to find comfort was beyond heart wrenching. We decided to sit in our shower and allow the steam to work its way through her tiny lungs and clear out her airways. I sat on the built-in bench, the water aimed directly at the floor, and James placed Hope in my arms.

"You should see if she will latch onto you," he suggested. Hope's head faced my bare chest and her mouth hovered close to my exposed nipple.

"No, that would be weird!" I said, not giving the idea any thought. She had only used nipples from a bottle. "She probably wouldn't even recognize my fake boobs anyway."

"Well, your nipples aren't fake," James said, with a shrug.

"What if she doesn't latch?" I asked. If she didn't, I worried I would feel rejected and left to question if we shared a connection. I'd been doing my best to distance myself from these fears since the moment she was born.

"Yeah, but what if she does?" he said and held my gaze.

I looked at Hope, knowing I had a choice and regardless of what she did, I also could choose how to respond. I wouldn't let myself slide into a spiral if she didn't latch, but how special would it be if she did?

I moved my nipple slightly, placing it directly in front of her mouth. Her expression changed, and her lips began to gently root against my skin when suddenly, she latched onto my nipple and instinctively started sucking. I couldn't feel a thing and I didn't let her linger long, but right then, every fear I'd ever had about not bonding with Hope disappeared. There was no doubt she knew I was her mom.

EPILOGUE

The night Hope was born, Brianna was given medications to treat what the doctors thought was pre-eclampsia, her blood pressure still higher than they would have liked to see. She was set to be released from the hospital and begin her recovery with Ben and her kids the following day.

Before being discharged, she experienced an uncomfortable wheezing in her chest, and the nurses examined her, listening for anything of concern. Hearing nothing in her lungs, they advised her to return to the hospital if her symptoms persisted or worsened. She went home, feeling a bit sore from the delivery and was happily welcomed by her family, while James and I remained in the hospital with Hope.

That evening, while trying to sleep, her heart began to race and the wheezing in her chest became noticeably worse. Initially worried she somehow contracted COVID in the hospital, she used an at-home oximeter and blood pressure cuff to check her vitals. Her oxygen level was in the high eighties, and her blood pressure was higher than when she left the hospital. Her gut told her something wasn't right, and she left her family, kids still asleep, to go to the local emergency room (ER), located in a different hospital.

After examining her and completing an EKG, the doctor and staff believed her symptoms were in line with her earlier diagnosis of pre-eclampsia. To be safe, they decided to do a chest x-ray which showed a buildup of some kind in her lungs and near her heart, leading them to request a chest MRI. Less than an hour passed between the x-ray and MRI, but the images from the MRI revealed a rapidly changing and scary scene. Her lungs and heart filled with fluids at an alarming rate.

The ER called Dr. Barney, who immediately recommended she be seen by a cardiologist. She was taken by ambulance back to the hospital she'd been discharged from less than twenty-four hours earlier. In the ambulance, the emergency medical technician informed her she'd been at a highly dangerous risk of having a heart attack or stroke at any moment and would likely be admitted to the hospital for several days. Hearing this news completely derailed all hope she'd had of spending time with her family while recovering from having just given birth.

Her arrival to the cardiology unit was a stark contrast to the labor and delivery ward she'd recently left. The staff quickly debriefed her about what was happening, asked her for her living will, and even gave directions to the chapel, if she felt the need to go pray. Having not been prepared for this complication, she hadn't packed an overnight bag or any supplies.

The cardiologist ran an echocardiogram, a test using sound waves to produce images of the heart's valves and chambers to evaluate pumping action and blood flow. The test showed although blood was pumping into her heart normally, it was only pumping blood out at a rate of twenty percent. She was diagnosed with cardiomyopathy, also known as heart failure.

At first, the doctors believed this condition had been caused by the stress of her pregnancy and delivery of Hope. Heart failure is a common risk among pregnant women and is called perinatal/postpartum cardiomyopathy. Having no known cause, it is a rare condition that typically begins during the final month of pregnancy and can last up to five months following delivery.

With this diagnosis, Brianna remained in the hospital while the doctors attempted to rid her body of extra fluids building in her heart and lungs, causing her heart to work harder. After two days of no improvement to her heart rate, now triple the rate it was when she was first admitted, the doctors began looking for other reasons this could be happening. Another MRI was ordered, but it took about five days to find the right combination of medications to slow her pulse enough to effectively complete the test.

Once stabilized through her new cocktail of medications, she was able to go home, but was required to wear a defibrillator due to her high risk of heart attack or stroke. She was forced to stay inactive and wasn't even allowed to pick up either of her kids, now two and a half.

The guilt James and I felt over this revelation was something even having a healthy newborn couldn't assuage. We grappled with the impact this condition would have on her and her family for the rest of her life...not to mention how dangerously close she had been to something catastrophic happening throughout her entire pregnancy, but mostly, during labor.

It didn't take long for our army of support to wrap their arms around Brianna and hold her in their embrace. From meals, house-cleaning, babysitting, and a GoFundMe account, the love and compassion from those in our circle, as well as those she relied on during her own struggles with infertility, were nothing short of amazing.

Over the next several months, after numerous visits with specialists and constant adjustments to medications she would be required to take for the rest of her life, it was determined, through genetic testing, that Brianna had been living with a heart defect her entire life. If she hadn't given birth to Hope, it might have gone undetected.

Hearing this news was not easy. It meant she would have to closely monitor her heart health for the rest of her life. Additionally, her kids were able to be tested, and as a result, found they were positive for this condition as well. Although scary, the knowledge would help all of them live a healthier and more informed life.

Learning of her diagnosis brought me closer to her than I even imagined was possible. We both had genetic conditions that could have undoubtedly brought our lives to an early end if not discovered and monitored over time.

But the most miraculous connection Brianna and I will forever share is both of our lives were saved by Hope.